SMARTER BALANCED

GRADE 3

By Gayle Campbell, MA, MAT, a

BARRON'S

Acknowledgments

I would like to dedicate this book to the Nevada Mathematics Project Teachers. I am honored to meet such dedicated teachers who work hard to help their students learn math. I would like to thank my husband Scott Lamberg for his love and support and also my son Zack. Zack helped me edit this manuscript and provided useful feedback from a kid's perspective. I would also like to thank Ms. Mary Magee and her third-grade students who provided great insight and feedback as I developed this manuscript. Finally, I would like to thank Wayne Barr for his encouragement, support, and constructive feedback through my writing process. Kristen Girardi provided constructive feedback as well. I am grateful to my Nevada math project team members Ed Keppelman, Peggy Lakey, Travis Olson, Jeff Shih, Lucy Gillette, Denise Trakas, Marissa McClish, Tina Baer, Steven Demelin, and Craig Wall. We explored the standards and assessments together as a team along with the project teachers. We learned from the teachers as well. Our ultimate goal is to support students to learn math.

—Teruni Lamberg

I would like to dedicate this book to students and families who endeavor to be creative and skillful learners in the realm of standards-based teaching and learning. I would like to thank my husband Ryan Campbell for his particular love and wordy patience, and also my children Reed, Lucy, and Sage, for their understanding and encouragement, especially Lucy who gave her personal feedback from a student's perspective. I would also like to acknowledge my third-grade classes at Duffy who have worked hard to prepare themselves to be critical thinkers and express themselves in writing. Finally, I would like to thank Kristen Girardi who provided suggestions and deadlines, and Wayne Barr for his humor and personal connection throughout this process. My hope is that this book will help parents and families understand that children in third grade can read critically, engage with texts actively, and respond meaningfully in writing.

—Gayle Campbell

All inquiries should be addressed to:
Barron's Educational Series, Inc.
250 Wireless Boulevard
Hauppauge, NY 11788
www.barronseduc.com

ISBN: 978-1-4380-0935-3

Library of Congress Control Number: 2016949824

Date of Manufacture: October 2016
Manufactured by: B11R11

Printed in the United States of America
9 8 7 6 5 4 3 2 1

10%
POST-CONSUMER
WASTE
Paper contains a minimum
of 10% post-consumer
waste (PCW). Paper used
in this book was derived
from certified, sustainable
forestlands.

Contents

PART ONE
English Language Arts

What Every 3rd Grader Needs to Know About the Smarter Balanced Grade 3 ELA Exam

Whatever your ponderings, thoughts, and feels are about standardized testing, it is a reality that your third-grade child will be taking the Smarter Balanced Assessment Consortium (SBAC) testing series. As an experienced third-grade teacher, I have administered this test. As a parent, I also have had a third-grade child take the test. In both these roles, I have gleaned some incite and noticed how children react to being "put to the test." Children are indeed more resilient and capable than you could ever imagine. Nonetheless, it is quite daunting to consider that your eight or nine year old will take on a task of this magnitude. This guide will take you on a small journey to prepare your child for taking this *new* kind of test, assuaging both your potential anxiety and his or her curiosity of the unknown. On this journey, you and your child will encounter two cities: Digitalville and Responderland.

Digitalville: Computers/iPads/Laptops

> Learn the basics of typing
> Become familiar with navigation tools, such as clicking between two windows
> Practice swiping/clicking a mouse pad and/or mouse or touchpad
> Get used to using headphones

Responderland: Reading/Comprehending/Responding

> Learn how to calmly troubleshoot on the spot
> Practice reading text carefully, or with purpose
> Hear from a student who has taken the test
> Learn to effectively highlight text or take notes
> Incorporate text in responses
> Respond in complete sentences and answer the question asked, not just stating what's on your mind
> Negotiate time management and frustration levels
> Practice skills by taking sample tests

As we visit these two neighboring cities, I will use some actual text, the vehicle by which we will practice the skills in each city. Encourage your child to put pencil to paper and mark these pages, as truly engaged readers will always do when encountering something new. Have a set of sticky notes on hand, as well! Writing, drawing, underlining, and commenting will help your child remember the key details, and allow them to comprehensively read and respond critically to a text. A reference to the Common Core Standards (CCS) is also included in the Appendix, so that as parents, you can see the correlation between the classroom curriculum and the SBAC testing, both of which are guided by the CCS.

Keep in mind your child will be using all of the above skills simultaneously! Let's gear up and get on our way!

Mission Control: Typing Tips

Before your child even thinks about taking the SBAC testing series, it is vital that he or she knows the basics about typing. It is a digital world in which we live, but most third graders are not experienced with typing! Many children have access to iPads, tablets, cellular phones, and all sorts of "swiping" devices. Some students like using an iPad to type, but the keyboard is often not ideal for typing effectively.

On the SBAC, students will need to type their responses. This can be the biggest hindrance for students to tackle during the testing situation. For some students, just approaching a computer and trying to find the keys is daunting. Students resort to "hunting and pecking," and typing becomes a time-consuming scavenger hunt, that increases test anxiety and detracts from the task at hand, which is to show they are critical thinkers and able to interact and respond to texts in meaningful ways.

Your child's school district should have a simple typing program for students to practice using the "home row" or typing commonly used words. It is not a requirement for students to use the "home row," as many parents were taught, but it is definitely helpful.

Certainly, your eight or nine year old will not become an expert typist by the time he or she takes the SBAC test, and you should not expect your child to type as fast as a grown-up! However, any practice is helpful. Keep in mind that a third grader (who has practiced typing) can type an average of 10–15 words per minute.

My school district has used *Type to Learn* products and *Typing Pal*. There is a district subscription for these types of programs. Families can also subscribe to these programs from home. I recommend your child practice typing 15–20 minutes per week. Students catch on quickly, and the great benefit is that typing is a lifelong skill.

When selecting a free typing program, make sure the keyboard suggested is the QWERTY keyboard, so that students are practicing on the same keyboard that they will be using for the test. I prefer the more straightforward typing sites over the game-like sites. Real typing is not a game, and typing responses to questions on the SBAC will certainly not feel like a game to your child.

There are many free online typing resources. Below are a few examples:

- *www.typing.com*
- *www.learninggamesforkids.com/keyboarding_games.html*
- *www.typing-lessons.org/*
- *www.speedtypingonline.com/typing-test*

You will need to show your child how to find frequently used keys. For instance, after showing the location of the shift keys, you might say, "Hold down the shift key, and keep holding it down until you press the letter or the key you want. Then, release the shift key."

ESSENTIAL KEYS FOR YOUR CHILD TO KNOW AND PRACTICE

> Finding the **spacebar** and using it to space words and adding a space after a comma or period

> Locating the **comma [,]** and **period [.]** keys

> Knowing the difference between and location of **backspace**, **delete**, and **enter**

> Using the **shift** key for capital letters at the beginning of sentences and of proper nouns (names of people, places, and things)

> Using the **shift** key for **quotation marks [" "]**, the **question mark [?]**, and the **exclamation point [!]**

> Showing how to underline titles

> Using the **direction keys**, moving the **cursor**, and **scrolling** up and down are all crucial tools when answering questions on the SBAC

In addition, knowing how to use the **tab key** and how to click between two windows at once is very helpful. The constructed responses, or open-ended responses, often require students to click on the writing/responding portion, and at the same time reread the text(s) offered to provide evidence in their writing. However, it is also possible for your child to write the response by hand, and then type what was handwritten. While this may seem like double-work, it is often how students work through the writing process when not being tested. Because the SBAC series is not timed, it is reasonable that students could take the time to organize their thoughts on paper, like traditional writing on demand with paper and pencil, and then transfer their writing into typing. For some students, thinking, typing, revising, and clicking between windows is too overstimulating. This could be another reason to write first and type second.

Whichever method your child chooses to use when responding to texts on the SBAC, it is a good idea to emphasize that there is more than one way to get the job done. He or she needs to organize his or her thoughts, answer questions based on the text provided, and construct a meaningful response. Using scratch paper, notes, Post-It Power (see Chapter 2), and handwritten planning sheets/graphic organizers are all tools your child would use in a classroom setting. I use these tools in my classroom to determine how my students think, plan, and write. Collaborating with your child's teacher is also a smart plan, so that you can both prepare your child to do his or her best.

How Do We Work This Thing? Navigation Tools

While typing on the computer keyboard is one task that can hinder students when taking the SBAC testing series, using the navigation tools might also cause them some consternation! Practice with moving the cursor with the mouse or touchpad to the correct icon will help students learn to quickly access the tools and put them to use.

I would strongly suggest consulting the SBAC practice testing website: *http://sbac.portal.airast.org/practice-test/*. You can access the practice test directly with the following address: *https://practice.smarterbalanced.org/student/*. I encourage you to take the practice test yourself. Doing this will not only give you a sense of what your child will have to negotiate when taking the test, but it may also inspire you to consider supplemental readings or experiences for your child. No matter how informative an excerpt of writing on the SBAC may be, one cannot underestimate the power of diverse background knowledge for students. Taking the test yourself, and experiencing the range and level of text rigor, will help you address potential gaps in your child's schema or background knowledge.

Students should absolutely take the practice test. Students often learn by actually doing much faster and more efficiently than by reading about how to do something. The practice test allows your child to choose the grade and type of test. He or she will then be able experiment with clicking between windows and using the tools SBAC provides for use during the actual test. The list is rather dense, so it may not be overtly clear how students would use these tools, and your child's teacher most likely will not take up too much learning time going through all these buttons and clicks. There has to be a balance between preparing third graders for a computer-based test, and focusing only on the logistics of taking the test.

The most useful tools for the students to use while taking the test are the "zoom" function, the "arrow" buttons, and the "pause" button. Different schools have different rules for using all these tools. Make sure, if you give parental advice about which tools your child should use, that it is in line with what his or her teacher has instructed.

Included within this SBAC site is a page that takes students through all the options they will have available to them while taking the test. Students will be asked to highlight a piece of text, and then drag it to the correct order in which it occurs within a passage. They will have to decide how a certain piece of text might fit in a passage. I highly recommend watching the clicking and dragging videos on the parent and student tutorial site found here: *http://ct.portal.airast.org/item-type-tutorials/*.

In these tutorials, students can see what needs to be done, but they still may not be able to maneuver selecting text, highlighting text, and then moving text. This takes practice. Again, for some students this comes easily, but for others, it is asking them to learn far too many layers of technology on top of the ultimate goal, which is to answer a reading comprehension question thoughtfully and critically. It is important to note, however, that many districts do not give students access to all the "bells and whistles" available when taking the test. They do not want to distract them from the task at hand. Still, it is helpful to check out the site and experiment with the options: *https://demo.tds.airast.org/eqtutorial/*.

If your child has an IEP (Individualized Education Plan) or a special education mandated 504 plan, it is imperative that the plans are followed for equity across all students taking the test. The classroom teacher, in conjunction with the Pupil Services Team at your school, will have information on any accommodations made for your child while taking the test. The accommodations are diverse and completely dependent upon the student's individual needs. Realize that students with specialized plans have been identified through a lengthy and specific process at their schools, regardless of standardized computer-based testing.

Lastly, students should never submit their test until they have consulted with a teacher. The SBAC testing series is still quite new, and all assessments (and test takers) are imperfect. It is reasonable that third graders ask their teachers to make sure they are on the right test, on the correct screen, and they have given their best effort before hitting the "submit" button.

Help! I Can't Find It! Clicking with the Mouse or Touchpad

When the SBAC test is administered, many students will be provided with a laptop or desktop with which they are familiar. However, electronic devices are supplied according to availability, and it is possible your child may be asked to use a computer that he or she is not familiar with. Therefore, you should encourage your child to use other computers so that he or she is familiar with the different sensitivities of touchpads and so on. While many of these electronic acts are intuitive, for some students, especially those who have only been using an iPad or tablet at home, it will take some getting used to maneuvering a mouse or using two fingers to control a touchpad in order to get it to respond accurately.

Keep in mind that while typing, the heals of the hands will often rest on the touchpad. This almost always causes the cursor to jump to another location, highlight an unintended piece of text, or move text where the child didn't intend it to go. Children are often looking at the keys to locate each letter, so they will not quickly see the relocation of text until they finally look up, and then are often unsure how to fix it. Sometimes this causes panic.

During a test, I have heard students say, "I just typed this whole paragraph and now it disappeared!" Or, "I know I typed my answer in the box, but now that answer is in another question. How did it get there?" It is frustrating for both teachers and students. Teachers will sometimes be able to see what the student has done, but they are unable to help during the test. Teachers cannot retype or manipulate ANY portion of the SBAC test. All we can say to your child is to "Do your best." "Take a deep breath." "Delete what you do not want, and retype what you want." Encourage your child to look up when typing the responses every sentence or two. Most students will be able to see what happened to the text if they are paying attention more readily.

Using various devices at home, at school, or at your public library will help your child acclimate to the different sensitivities required when using a mouse or a touchpad. While engaging your child in these activities, encourage them to type, highlight, and move text, instead of merely playing a computer game. Typing a letter to a loved one, composing a simple poem, or writing a journal entry of the day's events will account for some substantial text that can be edited using a mouse or touchpad. Practice with copying and cutting and pasting are also skills that the average third grader will benefit from learning, as it will acclimate them to using these technological tasks. Being aware of what is happening at their fingertips and on screen will alleviate undue stress.

You Can't Hear Me Singing, Right? Listening Skills

A very small portion of the Smarter Balanced Consortium testing series may include listening to a story or article. Students will be expected to listen to the text, and then respond to questions using the information they learned. As with any test, there are the actual logistics of taking the test, and then there are the reading comprehension skills that the test is supposed to be evaluating. The same goes for using headphones.

When administering the test, situations arise like headphones becoming unplugged, or that there are three different ways to adjust the volume! Teachers and students have to make sure that if the headphones have a volume control, it has to be unmuted and turned on. A second way to check volume is to see if the settings control panel is set to unmuted and then adjust the volume. And finally, a third way to adjust volume is to use the actual function keys on the keyboard. All three of these volume controls need to be tested. It will save a considerable amount of time if you train your child how to do this, as it takes a lot of explaining and showing on the actual computer being used on test day. It's quick when done one-on-one, but multiply that by a couple of minutes by an entire class of third graders, and that couple of minutes turns into a 30–45 minute venture! Working through some of these computer-related tasks with your child will serve both the students and teachers on test day!

The second best way to help your child listen to text carefully, or with purpose, is to give them practice with oral directions. Specifically, children need to develop their listening skills by following multi-step directions. There are many ways to do this at home. Every day teachers give students directions for every learning job in the classroom. Most write down the directions, or they have a handout listing the steps involved in accomplishing an academic task. What is more difficult is having students listen to a set of directions, and then having the students follow them on paper.

Here is an example to share with your child. **Read the following paragraph aloud.** Then, ask your child to answer the questions below.

Chatty Mammals

In many ways, you are just like the more than 30 species of dolphins that swim in the world's oceans and rivers. Dolphins are mammals, like you are, and must swim to the surface to breathe air. Just as you might, they team up in pods, or groups, to accomplish tasks. And they're smart.

They also talk to each other. Starting from birth, dolphins squawk, whistle, click, and squeak. "Sometimes one dolphin will vocalize and then another will seem to answer," says Sara Waller, who studies bottlenose dolphins off the California coast. "And sometimes members of a pod vocalize in different patterns at the same time, much like many people chattering at a party." And just as you gesture and change facial expressions as you talk, dolphins communicate nonverbally through body postures, jaw claps, bubble blowing, and fin caresses.

Question: Who is "chatty" in this article?

Answer: Dolphins are chatty in this article.

Question: What do you think "vocalize" means?

Answer: Vocalize means to communicate using sounds like talking or whistling.

Question: How do you communicate like a dolphin?

Answer: I communicate like a dolphin when I talk, or whistle, or use motions to show what I'm trying to say.

Question: Name three ways a dolphin can communicate.

Answer: Three ways a dolphin can communicate are by blowing bubbles, caressing a fin, or squeaking. (There are many more listed in the article.)

It would also be helpful to have your child listen to a TV or radio commercial or news clip, and then ask what the point of the commercial or news story was.

Questions you could ask about a commercial:

- [ ] What was the name of the company?
- [ ] What was the company trying to sell?
- [ ] How would owning the product benefit your life?
- [ ] Why would someone want to purchase what was being sold in the commercial?
- [ ] How is the product similar to or different from any other product you either already own or know is already available?

Questions you could ask about a news story:

- [ ] Where is the location of the story?
- [ ] What is the main idea of the news story?
- [ ] What are three details you remember from the story?
- [ ] What problem does the newscaster highlight?
- [ ] What, if any, solutions are given in the story? Who is affected by the story?

While headphones are the "Digitalville" part of this chapter, it is crucial that listening skills are the focus. It is also possible to have children answer questions about a recorded article or story in a speak-to-text format, or have them type their answers. The issues with the headphones should be able to work themselves out if children are taught some self-help skills when using a computer in a testing situation.

What about the singing? Well, if you have ever been around students with headphones on, you will know that they forget others can hear them. It is typical for a classroom teacher to hear children talking or singing to themselves when wearing headphones, completely unaware that others can hear them. This humorous situation reminds us that these are young children taking a test. It would be a great idea if you reminded your child that others can hear them, even if others cannot hear what is playing in the headphones. Yes, we *can* hear you singing!

I Have a Co-Pilot: Troubleshooting with Calm

There are some simple ways to deal with frustration. A good night's sleep and a hearty breakfast will set your child up for success in anything he or she does. Help your child practice mindfulness and breathing exercises to reduce anxiety and put things into perspective. Because many students will be taking the test at the same time, it is expected that there will be technological difficulties, clogged Wi-Fi paths, and student error. All sorts of things can happen when little fingers type, click, highlight, move, relocate, and read text while under the stress of testing. It is important to emphasize that your child does not need to focus on the technology over the reading and responding to text. Of course, this is easier said than done, but I cannot stress (pun intended) enough that the technology should only be the tool used to answer questions on the test, especially because exposure to using a computer is not consistent across all children, classrooms, or school districts. Practicing mindfulness also benefits parents and teachers as we help navigate the demands on our students to show what they know in a testing situation.

Earlier we addressed the technological concerns, now we will focus on mindfulness. Students will benefit in all their learning if there is a focus on mindfulness. Breathing and bringing oneself to the moment of the breath quickly reminds students to focus on their own bodies in a calm way. The trick is to get students to realize this while they are under the stress of testing. I have students stretch and breathe just before testing begins so that activity (or lack thereof) serves as a gentle reminder to calm down. I can then refer to those moments during the test. While there is a set of teacher instructions, it is okay to say to a struggling or befuddled student, "You got this." "You're doing great." "Read it again." "Follow the directions carefully." And, "Take a breath or two."

It is in the breathing that children find the space they need to focus their attention, control their mental distractions, and move positively through a learning task. The routine may go something like this:

- Sit comfortably in your chair. Feet flat on the ground. Hands resting in your lap.
- Breathe in through your nose for 3 counts.
- Sneak in one more breath.
- Exhale through your mouth for 4 counts.

More kinesthetic children would need to add arms to the breathing. In that case, I would ask students to stand up, and inhale as they bring their arms up over their heads. Then, exhale as they bring their arms back to their sides. They could even do a bend of their knees as they start inhaling. I would follow the routine three times.

As students are taking the SBA, teachers will monitor their progress and anxiety levels. When a teacher notices a student is checking out, or eyes start wandering, or there is no activity (reading, typing, using scratch paper), it is time to re-engage. Children at this age need a moment to take a break—get a drink of water, walk to the bathroom, or stretch—so that they can re-focus for the test. My school also gives out mints to students. It has been suggested for years that mint encourages mental acuity, and the students feel like they're getting a treat. Even better. It is not often that students are handed a piece of candy from their teacher, so the simplicity of providing a mint becomes even more positive.

After all the skills are practiced, and the pragmatics of the test are managed, students will still feel frustrated given the nature of the test. Some students will be absolutely focused the entire time, while other students will not know when or how to start the test, and still others will race through the test and claim they are ready to submit before they have even shown their best effort! To combat these aforementioned issues, students should be encouraged to work on academic tasks independently.

Part of learning something new is the struggle that is embedded within the new learning itself. While the topics being addressed on the SBAC test are not necessarily new, responding to the questions on a computer is new, and therefore, students should practice typing responses to questions. Also, when reading the interview transcript with an actual student who has taken the test (page 14), you will notice she mentions taking "pauses." In alignment with the SBAC online documents, there is a "pause" feature when taking the test. Students can tap this button, with teacher permission, to give themselves a break. The longest pause a student can take is 20 minutes. I would not advise a student to click on the "pause" button independently, or to use the full 20 minutes when permission is granted. However, if it is deemed beneficial for a student to take a small break, whether to use the bathroom, take a quick walk, or just to take some time away from the test, it is recommended that they do so. Again, that is something that is available to students, but only with teacher permission. Keep in mind, the teacher has to follow school district guidelines within the SBAC instruction manual, so it is not for a student to decide when he or she needs a break. The student must ask for permission, or if the teacher feels that the student may need a few minutes to rejuvenate his or her energy and refocus on the SBAC test, a break will be suggested.

Teachers will also take care of separating students so that they have their own little "office." Sometimes there are privacy partitions on desks and sometimes desks are moved to various locations around the room. Teachers also provide pencils, scratch paper, and a comforting presence. I always do "chair yoga" and some mindful breathing to create a relaxed atmosphere for students. I remind them that while this testing is "a big deal," it is also just one measure of how they have been learning all year, just one opportunity to show what they know individually, and that each one of them is valued as a whole person. In previous years, students in my class have thought taking the test was fun! They feel important knowing that their answers will be considered and valued. Assessments are just one part of showing what they know as third graders.

Interview with a Student Who Has Taken the SBAC

How does an actual student feel about taking the SBAC test? Whatever parents and teachers may think about testing, or do to prepare students for testing, the reality is that it is the students themselves who are sitting in front of a screen, reading passages, accessing previously learned skills and strategies, maneuvering through the test, and then negotiating their typing skills and reading comprehension responses. Below is an interview with a fifth grader who answered the following questions about when she took the SBAC as a third grader.

Question: How did you feel when you were about to take the SBAC for the first time?

Student: I felt pretty nervous because I didn't know what was going to happen. Even after taking the practice test, I still didn't feel very pumped up about it because it probably was going to be graded, so I didn't want to get any wrong.

Question: Do you think most students felt like you did?

Student: I think they felt that way because they had never taken this type of test before. After the test, a lot of students were saying that they were super nervous about it because they did not want to get a bad grade or do poorly on the test.

Question: How did your teacher prepare you for taking the test? What kinds of activities did you do in order to get ready before the SBAC?

Student: My teacher prepared me for taking the test by doing the practice test that was available online. Each student did a different test. We watched a video with the whole class to learn how to use the tools. Like increasing and decreasing the size of the font, highlighting text, and using the flag button, so you could flag your spot and go back to it later.

Question: How well does the average third grader need to type to accomplish taking the SBAC test?

Student: We did not have any typing practice, so we just used our fingers to search for the letters. It took a really long time. Because the test is not timed, it really didn't matter how long it took you to type.

Question: How easy can the average third grader navigate the tools on the SBAC test?

Student: We used the icons on the top of the screen to figure out what to do. It was very easy to figure out.

Question: Tell me about how the headphones were used during the test. Any tips?

Student: We used headphones during the test, and I recommend making sure both of your earpieces work. I also recommend having your volume on low, about three bars, so your volume doesn't disturb any other people who are taking the test. If you have headphones that don't work, and there are no more headphones in the classroom, you should go to the hallway, or take the test at a different time.

Question: What did you notice about time management when you or others were taking the test?

Student: I noticed that a lot of people finished quickly, and I think that was because they just pressed any random answer if they didn't know what the question was asking.

I think that half the class finished before me and half the class finished after me. I think that was because I reread the questions a lot and reread the passages to make sure I was understanding all the details included in the question.

Some people took three sessions, which were about an hour each to finish up their test. You have two sessions to finish the test in class, and if you didn't finish in those two sessions, you would have to go with another teacher in a different room, so you would miss what was going on in the classroom.

When you finished, you had to read a book. But before you finished, you had to raise your hand and ask the teacher to press the submit button.

Question: What was the easiest part of taking the test? Why?

Student: The easiest part of taking the test was when you could either increase or decrease the size of the font so you could see it better.

Question: What was the hardest part of taking the test? Why?

Student: The hardest part of taking the test was clicking the next button because you wouldn't know what was going to happen next if you were going to get it wrong, or if you were going to get it right. It was stressful because the words were very tricky in the questions. I didn't always know what to put in because the words were not making sense to me. I didn't know what the answer should look like.

Question: How frustrated did you notice students felt when taking the test?

Student: I noticed that when people got frustrated they either did some belly breaths where you put your hands on your belly and you just breathe with your eyes closed. Or, they just put their heads on their desk for a few minutes. I think it was the students that were taking their time and were on like # 20 when it was almost a full hour and they hadn't gotten a lot of problems done compared to how other students had.

Question: What made you feel the most successful when taking the test? Why?

Student: I felt most successful when taking the test when I did the multiple-choice questions because you could easily eliminate some of the answers if they didn't make sense while you were reading the passage and questions.

Highlighting and Coding the Text

One of the key tasks a third grader can do to delve into a text and actively engage with a text is to **highlight** or **code** the text. There are several different ways students are taught to do this, but I suggest the following ways, as I have seen success with these methods in both overachieving and less confident students. Many teachers have called similar ways of purposefully engaging with the text as "Reading is Thinking." I call it "Post-It Power," and it truly helps students decipher what they are reading and make meaningful connections with it. Students can use "Post-It Power" for fiction, nonfiction, and poetic texts.

Because the SBAC testing series is on the computer, using a Post-It, or sticky note, is the best way students can **code** the text. The SBAC testing series does have a **highlighting** feature for students to actually highlight the text while reading. There are two problems with this method: 1) students tend to over-highlight, and thereby make the process of highlighting ineffective; and 2) the highlighting only stays for one day, so if your child does not complete the writing task in one day, the highlighting will not carry over to the next day. This is both frustrating for students and teachers, as we see them working so hard on one day, only for it all to be gone the next. To alleviate this frustration, I suggest using slips of paper, Post-Its, or sticky notes to record their ideas. Of course, if one has practiced this in class, it will make the process much more automatic while taking the SBAC test.

What Is "Post-It Power?"

"Post-It Power" is a coding process I have developed that helps students read for meaning and purpose. I teach students eight different ways to respond to the text in the moment, so that when the time comes to talk or write about the text, they will remember where in the text they found specific information and ideas, or how they felt at a particular point in the text. I use basic symbols to encourage students to respond to the text, so there is minimal writing and more meaningful responding, which in a test-taking situation is helpful. Students can empower themselves by coding the text, and then feel prepared to answer the questions that follow.

When students are reading from a book or anthology that cannot be written in, I give them Post-Its on which to write the symbol they are thinking about in response to the text. They can then carefully read and mark up the text by close reading, and are prepared to talk about why they put that symbol next to the text. When students are reading a photocopy or magazine on which they can write directly, like *Time for Kids* or *Scholastic News*, I have them code the text by writing the symbol directly on the page. Students take ownership of their reading and responding, and then, in turn, find more success in responding to the text in their writing.

Since students will be reading the text on a computer, I encourage them to write the number of the paragraph they are reading on the Post-It, as well. Using "Post-It Power" also helps students take ownership of what they think about a text. In a testing situation, this reading strategy serves to lower stress levels, as students engage with the text by using pictures, and they can put the symbols where they think it is appropriate without worry that they are being evaluated in the moment. This is an incredibly helpful strategy that helps students stay organized in their thinking and alleviates text anxiety.

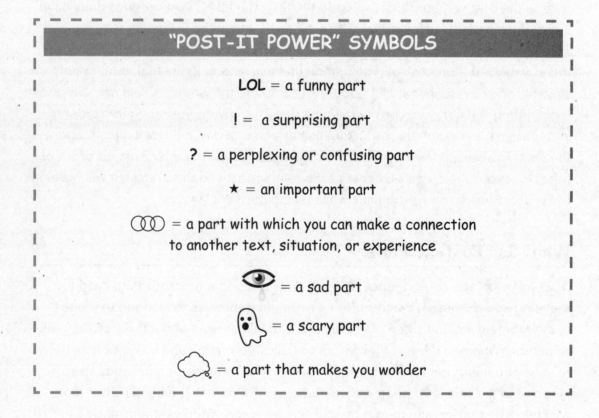

"POST-IT POWER" SYMBOLS

LOL = a funny part

! = a surprising part

? = a perplexing or confusing part

★ = an important part

⬤⬤⬤ = a part with which you can make a connection to another text, situation, or experience

👁 = a sad part

👻 = a scary part

☁ = a part that makes you wonder

Once a student has coded the text using "Post-It Power," including the paragraph or stanza number on each Post-It, then, and only then, can the student use a highlighter to make note of the Post-Its that help answer the questions being asked.

Using the Post-Its empowers students to take control over the text. Because they can decide what to write down as important, how to organize them, and how often they should use them, students take more ownership over their learning. Post-It Power creates a visual map of information, organizing first-look interpretations into thoughtful responses. By engaging in this process, students determine what is important in the text, narrow their focus, and allow for more clarity and specificity of their responses, as well as leave a trail of reminders about key sentences or words that might support their evidence. Using Post-It Power is not the only reading strategy that allows students to take ownership of the text, but it is one that is accessible, relatively simple to employ, and is effective in deepening student understanding of the text.

Responding in Full Sentences and Answering the Question Asked

Let's take a look at a nonfiction text. Students may encounter a nonfiction text that is multifaceted and includes a diverse array of text features like the one on page 22. The reading level may be elevated from third grade, so it is advantageous to practice with a text that is written for a slightly older set of readers, as your child can use the highlighting, coding, and responding techniques before sitting down to take the official test.

The text I have included is from a popular kid-friendly website that highlights current news stories of interest to students from grades 3 to 12. I use it frequently in class, and find that students like the engaging topics, as well as the ability of the site to draw in readers to more scientific subjects. Often, students remark how they never realized something before, or that they now understand why something happens after reading an article on the news site. While parents and teachers would consider the SBAC test to be an evaluation of knowledge applied, students often tell me what they have learned new from reading something on the test! If presented without the stressful high stakes layer, the testing questions will absolutely be seen by students as another opportunity to learn something new as they respond to questions.

One of the biggest issues I see when students respond to any reading comprehension question is that they forget to answer in a full sentence. There is an old reminder for that, which is quite simple: TTQA or Turn the Question Around. There are many gimmicks and mnemonic devices that trigger the memory to do this, but I believe the quickest to the point the better. Also, TTQA can be written very quickly on a piece of scratch paper, which every child will have while taking the SBAC test, and then the reference can be made each time a written response is expected.

Read the text below, and try the questions that follow with your child. Notice how easy it is to respond to the text by restating the question, a key to helping students both answer the question being asked and responding in full sentences.

Nonfiction Text

Practice Questions

(Answers can be found on pages 57–58.)

Go Ahead and Let Out That Long Sigh—It's Good for You!

Just when we think there couldn't possibly be any more mysteries left to solve about the human **anatomy**, there comes another discovery. This one has to do with sighing. It turns out that the involuntary **reflex** that is generally associated with sadness or despair is **crucial** to our well-being. That is why researchers at the University of California, Los Angeles and Stanford University were determined to find out what triggers the **spontaneous** action, without which our lungs would collapse!

A sigh is just a deep breath which starts out as a normal breath but extends when we inhale more air before letting it out. And while you may not realize it, most of us sigh once about every five minutes, or approximately twelve times an hour, regardless of whether we are sad or depressed.

To understand why, we need to learn a little about how the lungs function. As you are probably aware, our lungs are comprised of many branches or **bronchioles** each of which divides into millions of tiny sacs called **alveoli**. The alveolus (singular for alveoli) is where the respiratory system comes in contact with the **circulatory** system and conducts the all-important exchange of oxygen and carbon dioxide. The sacs inflate and collapse as we breathe in and out. However, the alveoli need to be inflated completely to avoid them from collapsing. Since that cannot be accomplished with just regular breathing, our body takes a deep breath or what we call a "sigh" every few minutes.

Though scientists have known this for many years, they had not been able to identify what triggers this **involuntary** life-sustaining reflex. However, two previous studies—one conducted by the University of California, Los Angeles and the other at Stanford University—had found the answer to half the puzzle. Now, thanks to a **collaboration** between the two institutions, the mystery has been finally solved.

The study conducted by Stanford researcher Mark Krasnow and his team had identified the 200 **neurons** in the brain cells that are responsible for releasing two **peptides**, protein fragments that allow the brain cells to "talk" to each other. What they could not figure out was which brain cells they were communicating with and more importantly what they were instructing them to do. Meanwhile, UCLA **neurology** professor Jack Feldman and his team had discovered that the same family of peptides (common to both mice and humans) were very involved in the part of the brain that controls breathing.

The two combined their knowledge to conduct further studies on mice. They discovered that the peptides triggered the nerve cells that activate the **rodent's** muscles, which in turn **instigate** the involuntary sighs. The researchers said that when they blocked one set of peptides, the mice sighed at half the rate. When the peptides were blocked completely, the mice stopped sighing altogether. **Conversely**, when the peptides were increased, the number of sighs went up substantially—from 40 times an hour to 400 times!

The study which was published in the digital edition of science journal, *Nature*, on February 8, opens the possibilities of new medications to help people with severe **respiratory** conditions. It will also assist in a more efficient design of life support systems. But most important of all, it gives us an **imperative** reason to sigh! So go ahead and let out a long deep one—it will do your body good!

As we go through this set of questions, the proposed answers on pages 57 and 58 will first be written without restating the question so that you can see the progression of simple to complex responses.

1. What important bodily function is *sighing* linked to?

----

2. **Part A.** What are alveoli?

   O A.   Branches of the lungs
   O B.   Tiny sacs of the lungs
   O C.   Scientific words for lungs
   O D.   Tiny breaths within the lungs

   Part B. Based on your answer to Part A, describe about how many alveoli are present in your lungs, and what they are able to do for your lungs.

   ----

3. How is sadness connected to sighing and breathing?

   ----

4. Why is the connection between the lungs and the brain important during sighing?

   ----

5. Explain why this discovery could be important in respiratory science.

Incorporating Text in Written Responses

Whether the task is to read a story or to read a couple of articles, students will be asked to read for important information in the text and use it to answer the questions.

The first thing your child will see when launching the ELA test will be a split screen. On the left will be the text to be read, and on the right will be the set of questions guiding the reading. I would suggest reading the viewable questions first, and then reading with a purpose to answer the questions. Because this is not a timed test, encourage your child to read the text more than once. A close reading ensures a more successful response to each question. Please emphasize to your child that taking this test is not a race. A thoughtful response is preferred over a rushed and incomplete response.

Using the highlighting tool provided on-screen, students can highlight as they read. A caveat to this, however, is that children of this age tend to highlight WAY more than they need to (see Chapter 2 for more information on highlighting). Also, the highlighting does not carry over to the next test session, which your child may need to complete this portion of the test.

I strongly suggest you encourage your child to use scratch paper to jot down notes and ideas. Teachers should provide scratch paper for this purpose. Teachers can save the scratch paper from day to day, so that students do not forget what their writing focus was. On the scratch paper, encourage your child to write down the main idea and key details if it is a nonfiction passage, or the main events and story elements if it is a fictional passage. Graphic organizers are tools students can use to familiarize themselves with organizing their thoughts. Invariably, your child's teacher will have used graphic organizers in teaching to the standards throughout the year. A reminder to your child to use a simple way to organize information will help provide structure, focus, and hopefully a sense of calm when responding to the text.

The questions on the test often contain academic vocabulary that students may or may not have had practice or exposure to. The following list will help your child feel more comfortable when taking the actual test.

HELPFUL VOCABULARY

> **Arrange**—put in a certain order
> **Author's message**—the central idea the *author is trying to convey, or show*
> **Conclusion**—two separate meanings may confuse children: 1) ending and 2) judgment (which may or may not be a fact) based on a particular set of reasons discussed in the text
> **Convey**—to show how something is understandable; to communicate an idea
> **Details**—also called "key details," these are ideas in the text that are specific to the main idea. These ideas "unlock" the main idea, and directly support it.
> **Inference**—an assumption or guess *based on evidence from the text*
> **Passage**—a selection or part of text
> **Support**—reinforce an idea *with facts from the text*
> **Events**—what happens in the story

Practice with Annotation

(Answers can be found on pages 59–61.)

Below is a text for your child to read and annotate using the Post-It Power symbols on page 18.

The people of the city of Baltese became obsessed with the elephant.

In the market square and in the ballrooms, in the stables and in the gaming houses, in the churches and in the squares, it was "the elephant, the elephant that came through the roof, the elephant conjured by the magician, the elephant that crippled the noblewoman."

The bakers of the city concocted a flat, oversized pastry and filled it with cream and sprinkled it with cinnamon and sugar and called the confection an elephant ear, and the people could not get enough of it.

The street vendors sold, for exorbitant prices, chunks of plaster that had fallen onto the stage when the elephant made her dramatic appearance. "Cataclysm!" the vendors shouted. "Mayhem! Possess the plaster of the disaster!"

The puppet shows in the public gardens featured elephants that came crashing onto the stage, crushing the other puppets beneath them, making the young children laugh and clap in delight and recognition.

From the pulpits of the churches, the preachers spoke about divine intervention, the surprises of fate, the wages of sin, and the dire consequences of magic gone afoul.

The elephant's dramatic and unexpected appearance changed the way the people of the city of Baltese spoke. If, for instance, a person was deeply surprised or moved, he or she would say, "I was, you understand, in the presence of the elephant."

As for the fortune tellers of the city, they were kept particularly busy. They gazed into their teacups and crystal balls. They read the palms of thousands of hands. They studied their cards and cleared their throats and predicted that amazing things were yet to come. If elephants could arrive without warning, then a dramatic shift had certainly occurred in the universe. The stars were aligning themselves for something even more spectacular: rest assured, rest assured.

Meanwhile, in the dance halls and in the ballrooms, the men and the women of the city, the low and the high, danced the same dance: a swaying, lumbering two-step called of course, the Elephant.

Everywhere, always, it was "the elephant, the elephant, the magician's elephant."

*   *   *

"It is absolutely ruining the social season," said the Countess Quintet to her husband. "It is all people will speak of. Why, it is as bad as a war. Actually, it is worse. At least with a war, there are well-dressed heroes capable of making interesting conversation. But what do we have here? Nothing, nothing but a smelly, loathsome beast, and yet people *will* insist on speaking of nothing else. I truly feel, I am quite certain, I am absolutely convinced, that I will lose my mind if I hear the word *elephant* one more time."

"Elephant," muttered the count.

"What did you say" said the countess. She whirled around and stared at her husband.

"Nothing," said the count.

"Something must be done," said the countess.

"Indeed," said Count Quintet, "and who will do it?"

"I beg your pardon?"

The count cleared his throat. "I only wanted to say, my dear, that you must admit that what occurred was, indeed, truly extraordinary."

1. Using details from the text, explain how you know what genre this book is.

----

2. Read the following sentence and the directions that follow.

The people of the city of Baltese were in awe of anything to do with the elephant.

Underline details that best support this conclusion.

"The bakers of the city concocted a flat, oversized pastry and filled it with cream and sprinkled it with cinnamon and sugar and called the confection an elephant ear, and the people could not get enough of it.

The elephant's dramatic and unexpected appearance changed the way the people of the city of Baltese spoke."

3. This question has two parts. First answer Part A. Then answer Part B.

Part A. Which sentence best describes the central idea of the passage?

- O A. The elephant would prefer to be with the Countess.
- O B. The Count believes the elephant is quite extraordinary.
- O C. The Countess is worried that the people of Baltese will have too many elephant ears.
- O D. The elephant has taken all the attention in the city of Baltese, and the Countess does not like that.

Part B. Which sentence from the passage best supports your answer to Part A?

- O A. The bakers of the city concocted a flat, oversized pastry and filled it with cream and sprinkled it with cinnamon and sugar and called the confection an elephant ear, and the people could not get enough of it.
- O B. The elephant's dramatic and unexpected appearance changed the way the people of the city of Baltese spoke.
- O C. I truly feel, I am quite certain, I am absolutely convinced, that I will lose my mind if I hear the word *elephant* one more time.
- O D. If elephants could arrive without warning, then a dramatic shift had certainly occurred in the universe.

4. Read the following sentence.

"The street vendors sold, for <u>exorbitant</u> prices, chunks of plaster that had fallen onto the stage when the elephant made her dramatic appearance."

What does the word <u>exorbitant</u> most likely mean?

- O A. Extra special
- O B. Very expensive
- O C. Extremely cheap
- O D. Really slippery

5. Arrange the following events in the correct order:

.... The fortune tellers made new predictions with their tea leaves.

.... An elephant fell through a roof unexpectedly.

.... The children laughed at puppets who re-enacted the appearance of the elephant.

.... A new phrase came into being that meant one was as surprised as when the elephant arrived in the city of Baltese.

.... People began talking about an elephant that seemed magical.

6. What inference can you make about what is important to the people of the city of Baltese? Use details from the passage to support your inference.

----

7. What could be the author's message in sharing this chapter? Be sure to use details from the passage to support your conclusion.

----

8. Why is including dialogue helpful in understanding the passage?
Pick **three** choices.

☐ A. It helps the reader understand that the people of the city of Baltese are dramatic.

☐ B. It helps the reader understand how important elephants are in general.

☐ C. It helps the reader understand why the children love the puppet show.

☐ D. It helps the reader understand what he or she would do if elephants came to his or her city.

☐ E. It helps the reader understand how the people of the city of Baltese believed the fortune tellers.

☐ F. It helps the reader understand why the bakers made the elephant ear.

9. Read the sentence from the passage.

"It is absolutely ruining the social season," said the Countess Quintet to her husband. "It is all people will speak of. Why, it is as bad as a war. Actually, it is worse. At least with a war, there are well-dressed heroes capable of making interesting conversation."

What does the phrase "absolutely ruining the social season" tell the reader about the Countess?

O A. The Countess likes all seasons, but prefers autumn and winter the best.

O B. The Countess wonders about conversation with heroes.

O C. The Countess would like to avoid an upcoming social war.

O D. The Countess puts a lot of stock in appearances and social status.

10. What do you suppose the Countess Quintet will do after this passage ends? Please use the ideas from the passage to write the next part of the story.

Reading for Purpose: Analyzing Poetry

Sometimes the SBAC test requires students to analyze poetry. Even if you and your child do not know the exact poetic form (a villanelle) of the poem on page 37, the expectation is for the student to figure out the meaning of words based on context clues, basic grammar, prefixes and suffixes, or figurative language such as similes and metaphors. The language in the poem can invite students to visualize images and connect with their own experiences. In a non-testing situation, encourage discussion when reading the poem together. Collaborative conversations are a great way for students to engage in the work of more sophisticated analysis without even realizing it! The poem on page 37 can be read as simply someone on a long drive or as something much deeper. Third graders often surprise us with how their imaginations can reveal a more mature understanding when given the opportunity to express their thinking in writing.

When reading poetry with third graders, the first thing to remember is to read it aloud. How do they do that in a testing situation? I encourage students to read with their lips moving, in less than a whisper. That slows them down and encourages them to "hear" the poem in their heads. Most students race through the poem and then claim, "I don't get it." They *do get it*. Students have great imaginations and the ability to make creative and realistic connections with the images in the poem.

I highly suggest that students make notes about each line as they read and re-read the poem. Some things they might also note are end rhymes, repetition of lines or sounds, images, and motifs (when a sound, word, color, image, or idea repeats itself in the poem at least three times). Remember, this is not a timed test. Your child will have plenty of time to write notes (see Chapter 2 for information on coding and making notes on the text) about his or her thoughts before writing a response. Also, if he or she makes an outline or jots down key sentences for the responses, he or she will feel more confident about typing them. Remind your child that all ideas about the poem must be grounded in the text. So, encourage him or her to pull out lines that seem important or are vivid depictions of an object or situation, and use that as textual evidence to support the claims.

HELPFUL VOCABULARY

> **Metaphor**—comparing two different things without using *like* or *as* to show a similar trait

  Example: My head is a tornado. (This could mean your thoughts are swirling so fast and crazy, a tornado is happening in your head! But, not actually!)

> **Simile**—comparing two different things using *like* or *as* to show a similar trait

  Example: Reed can't, but Lucy can swim as fast as a swordfish. (This could mean Lucy can swim so fast, she could compete with a swordfish, who swims fast!)

> **Theme**—the main argument or message of a text

  Example: A central theme of *Charlotte's Web* is friendship because it shows how Wilbur values Charlotte's friendship to feel accepted, loved, and then to save his life!

Practice Questions

(Answers can be found on pages 61–63.)

Answer the following questions based on the poem below.

The Drive

Driving gray lanes equidistant to you
Music plays popular songs of heartbreak
Imagining bare trees my band and crew

Winter always wonders at what is true
The lonely road is the freedom I take
Driving gray lanes equidistant to you

Slender branches reach up to gray sky clues
Melodic memories sit like a glass lake
Imagining bare trees my band and crew

The high clouds witness feelings of bland blue
Wishes like rock slides, steep and without shake
Driving gray lanes equidistant to you

Familiar routes under which wild geese flew
No one sees their feather's down is not fake
Imagining bare trees my band and crew

Singing why I travel this dismal view
Wondering where we'll meet at the rest break
Driving gray lanes equidistant to you
Imagining bare trees my band and crew

1. What does the word <u>equidistant</u> mean? Use context clues from the text.

   ○ A. Far away distance
   ○ B. Equal distance
   ○ C. Short distance
   ○ D. Unknown distance

2. What theme is the poet trying to convey in this poem?

   ○ A. Driving long distances is boring.
   ○ B. Traveling makes people want to sing.
   ○ C. Bare trees are skinny and straight, like memories.
   ○ D. Missing someone is like traveling long distances.

3. How does the repetition of some lines help portray the theme of the poem? Choose the best **two** responses.

   ☐ A. Repetition helps the reader remember the theme.
   ☐ B. Repetition shows the distance of the travel.
   ☐ C. Repetition emphasizes the loneliness the driver feels.
   ☐ D. Repetition hints at the exit the driver will take.

4. From what you know about patterns, what do you expect the rhyme scheme is for this poem?

   ○ A. ABC, ABC, ABC, ABC, ABC, ABCD
   ○ B. ABB, ABB, ABB, ABB, ABB, ABCD
   ○ C. ABA, ABA, ABA, ABA, ABA, ABAA
   ○ D. ABC, AAB, ABB, ABC, AAB, ABBA

5. What is a "glass lake?" Use context clues to make your decision.

   ○ A. A side view mirror
   ○ B. The windshield
   ○ C. A clear lake
   ○ D. A frozen lake

6. Using information from the text and your imagination, how can one compare "wishes" to "rock slides, steep and without shake?"

----

7. Based on this poem, list at least **two** characteristics of driving.

----

8. What could the "band and crew" be?

----

9. In what season can you infer this poem takes place? Use details from the poem to support your response.

English Language Arts Practice Test

CHAPTER
6

NOTE

On the actual exam, the format for longer text passages and questions will be different. Text passages and the questions that accompany them will be placed in a side-by-side, scrollable format. This side-by-side format will allow you to easily refer back to the passage for textual evidence.

(Answers can be found on pages 63–69.)

Directions: For questions 1 through 14, read *Unusual Friends*. Then, answer the questions.

Unusual Friends

2016 has been a terrific year so far. My mom always took me on her trips. We traveled everywhere together. We already had flown over to Colorado for a week of teaching and giving presentations on emergency medicine. We'd gone up to Canada for a little over a week to help train students there. We'd been so busy that we almost forgot we were to be leaving for Uganda in a couple of weeks. We had never been there before.

Going to the continent of Africa was so exciting. I simply couldn't wait to visit the villages and spend time with the African people and animals. In preparation, I decided to take a field trip up to the Portland Zoo to visit some native animals of Africa and get some tips as to what I should do in my spare time there. My trip to Portland was quite eventful to say the least. I gathered some information by talking with Elvira the African Elephant, Aeneas the gentle Antelope, and Musapo the African mouse.

Here's how my day at the zoo went:

"Excuse me," I said to the large, leathery, gray beast standing there taking a long drink from the pool of water before her.

41

"Gulp, gulp, gulp … yes?"

"Hi, I'm Moses, and I'm going to Uganda in a couple of weeks, and I was wondering if you could recommend some places to visit? I'm not going to have a lot of free time, but I would like to know what to look for." I sounded nervous because I was. She was so big, and I was so small. She dropped her long trunk back down into the water, lifted it to her mouth, and then began to speak, droplets of water dripping off of her lips.

"Uganda, huh. I haven't been there in years. I know what they say about us elephants, how we have good memories. But child, I've been here so long that I've forgotten what home looks like. Do you think you could just take some pictures of the countryside where I used to roam and bring them back for me? I know that's not very helpful, but I honestly can't remember. I was taken from there when I was a baby."

"Oh," I said, embarrassed that I had asked. "Sure, I can do that for you. What was your name again?"

"Elvira," she said. "I'm actually from Kenya, but Uganda is just east of Kenya, so pretty close. Thank you, Moses. Your kindness I won't forget. I promise."

After speaking with Elvira, I moved on to Aeneas the gentle Antelope, who stood grazing next to the fence in a lot bordering Elvira's.

"Excuse me. Hi. My name is Moses, and I'm going to Uganda in a couple of weeks, actually, and I was wondering if …"

"Squarsh, squarsh, squarsh, Uganda, huh?" he said, chomping on withered grass, staring at me with big eyes.

"Yes, Uganda," I repeated, "and I want to know if you have any recommendations for sightseeing? I'm going to take some scenic photos for Elvira over there, because when I asked her about what she remembered, she couldn't help me too much since she hasn't been there in years. I want to know what you think I should see in my free time. My mom is going to be busy treating patients and training medical students."

"Well, squarsh squarsh squarsh, I'd see, squarsh, the open plains if I were you, squarsh. I miss runnin', squarsh squarsh, all out in the open, squarsh."

"So, you just think I should go out on a safari tour?"

"Squarsh, yes, and see the rain forest, squarsh, too if you can. And if you can, bring me some real grass from over there. Squarsh squarsh, much appreciated, squarsh." He turned and left in search of more food.

Walking away from him, I thought, wow, Uganda must have a magnificent landscape for these animals to be talking about it with such good memories. I was getting excited about taking pictures and collecting some grasses to bring back to my newfound friends, but I didn't know how I could manage all this exploring by myself. Then I met Musapo the mouse. He wasn't stuck in a cage at all. In fact, I didn't find him. He found me.

"Excuse me," he said with a thick British-sounding accent. "I heard you're searching for information regarding Uganda. I could be of some assistance. I am Musapo of South Africa. But for ten years I worked as a tour guide taking groups all over Africa showing them the sights."

"Really?" I said, my interest piqued.

"Really."

"So where should I visit?" I asked.

"My friend, why don't you let me show you? I'm not locked up here in this zoo. I just hang out here for the free food. And I've been thinking about going back to Africa anyway. I'll come with you, and give you a personal tour of the highlights in Uganda."

"OK, but I'm going with my mom who's a doctor, and we will be visiting hospitals while we are there. Do you mind?"

"No, that's OK. What faith are you?" he asked.

"I'm a Christian, why?" I said.

"No problem. I am a Muslim, but I don't have problems with Christians. We're all here on this planet together. Are you okay with that?"

"Well, I agree with you, and anyway, my mom treats anyone, no matter what their faith, because she's a doctor," I said, leery of committing to anything at this point, as how would I explain sneaking this mouse on our trip to Uganda. "Could I have your cell number and call you back? I need to clear it with my mom. Deal?"

"Deal. Take all the time you need. Only let me know soon, so I can pack my bags." With that, he handed me his card and went on his way.

His card read:

Musapo Mouse

Tour Guide and Musician Extraordinaire

503-555-5555

email: musapo@mouse.mouse

After talking with my mom, she just smirked at me, gave me a hug, and said, "Sure, honey, you can bring your pet mouse with you, as long as he wears his scrubs in the hospitals."

I called him the next day. He was coming with us. I couldn't wait to have such an informative traveling companion.

1. Underline the sentence that best supports the idea that the narrator's mom understands that her child is using his imagination.

"After talking with my mom, she just smirked at me, gave me a hug, and said, 'Sure, honey, you can bring your pet mouse with you, as long as he wears his scrubs in the hospitals.'

I called him the next day. He was coming with us. I couldn't wait to have such an informative traveling companion."

2. Read the following sentences from the story.

" 'Well, I agree with you, and anyway, my mom treats anyone, no matter what their faith, because she's a doctor,' I said, leery of committing to anything at this point, as how would I explain sneaking this mouse on our trip to Uganda."

What does the use of the word leery suggest? Pick **two** choices.

☐ A. The narrator is concerned the mouse won't come with him.

☐ B. The narrator is worried that his mom won't believe he wants to bring a mouse with him.

☐ C. The narrator believes his mom is scared of mice.

☐ D. The narrator believes his mom will not let him in a hospital with a mouse.

☐ E. The narrator has never known a muslim before.

3. What conclusion can be drawn from the author's point of view? Support your answer with details from the passage.

----

4. Read the paragraph from the passage.

"2016 has been a terrific year so far. My mom always took me on her trips. We traveled everywhere together. We already had flown over to Colorado for a week of teaching and giving presentations on emergency medicine. We'd gone up to Canada for a little over a week to help train students there. We'd been so busy that we almost forgot we were to be leaving for Uganda in a couple of weeks. We had never been there before."

Why did the author choose to begin this story with this paragraph?
Select **two** choices.

☐ A. All the years prior to 2015 have been boring.

☐ B. The narrator must have been scared of flying.

☐ C. The author wanted to introduce the narrator and his mom.

☐ D. The reader will learn that the narrator's mom could be a doctor.

☐ E. Anyone who travels that much must be smart.

5. Re-read the following sentences from the passage.

"'I heard you're searching for information regarding Uganda. I could be of some assistance. I am Musapo of South Africa. But for ten years I worked as a tour guide taking groups all over Africa showing them the sights.'

'Really?' I said, my interest <u>piqued</u>."

What does the word <u>piqued</u> mean in this passage?

O A.   Moses would love to go to South Africa.

O B.   Musapo shows he is a trickster.

O C.   Musapo has a lot of information about traveling.

O D.   Moses is curious about how Musapo could help him.

6. Read the sentences from the passage.

"'<u>Squarsh</u>, yes, and see the rain forest, <u>squarsh</u>, too if you can. And if you can, bring me some real grass, from over there. <u>Squarsh</u> <u>squarsh</u>, much appreciated, <u>squarsh</u>.' He turned and left in search of more food."

Why does the author use the word <u>squarsh</u>?

O A.   To show the reader how grass sounds while growing under an antelope's feet

O B.   To show the reader how an antelope might sound while chewing and talking

O C.   To show the reader why antelopes talk with their mouths full

O D.   To show the reader why Moses is talking to an antelope

7. What can you infer about the narrator of this story? Is he really talking to animals? Is he using his imagination? Is Moses actually a human? Support your response with evidence from the story.

----

8. Read the following passage from the story. Locate the best synonyms for the sets of underlined words.

"Uganda, huh. I haven't been there in years. I know what they say about us elephants, how we have good memories. But child, I've been here so long that I <u>have forgotten</u> what home looks like. Do you think you could just take some <u>pictures</u> of the <u>countryside</u> where I used to <u>roam</u> and bring them back for me?"

- ○ A. Cannot recall, drawings, safari, run
- ○ B. Cannot recall, diagrams, home, run
- ○ C. Have fallen, photos, desert, wander
- ○ D. Cannot recall, photos, grasslands, wander

9. Rewrite the following sentence, correcting all seven grammatical errors.

I just coldnt beleive I was talking to a elefant. Oh wow I said to myself

----

----

10. This question has two parts. First answer Part A, and then answer Part B.

Part A. Which sentence best describes the lesson of the story?

- ○ A. Be wary of animals who talk at the Portland Zoo.
- ○ B. Always use your imagination to help you be open-minded.
- ○ C. Choose traveling over staying at home, so you don't get bored.
- ○ D. Be smart when you travel to hospitals in other countries.

Part B. Which sentence best supports your answer to Part A?

- ○ A. Imagination is always available to you, so you might as well use it.
- ○ B. Using your imagination is smart when you are faced with places, people, and situations you may not be familiar with.
- ○ C. Talking animals are a creative way to handle traveling to foreign places.
- ○ D. People in hospitals need visitors, even if they are imaginary.

11. Read the following sentence, and then follow the directions.

"Of the animals Moses met at the zoo, Musapo will be the best animal Moses could bring with him to Uganda."

Select the **two** details that best support this conclusion.

☐ A. Musapo is a mouse, so he can fit in Moses's pocket.

☐ B. Aeneas kept talking with her mouth full.

☐ C. Musapo worked as a tour guide, so he knows the best routes to take and places to go in Uganda.

☐ D. Elvira did not remember much about her homeland.

12. Why does the author mention Musapo's religion?

----

13. Arrange the events in the story in the order in which they occurred.

_____ Musapo meets Moses and decides to go with him on his trip to Uganda.

_____ Elvira tells Moses that she doesn't remember much about her homeland.

_____ Aeneas answers Moses's questions while talking with her mouth full.

_____ Moses visits the Portland Zoo to do some research.

_____ Moses's mom tells him it's okay to bring Musapo with him to Uganda.

14. Why is including dialogue important to understanding the passage?

Select **three** choices.

- ☐ A. It helps the reader know the reason Moses is going to Uganda.
- ☐ B. It helps the reader understand Moses's thinking.
- ☐ C. It helps the reader see how Moses's mom loves him and his imagination.
- ☐ D. It helps the reader understand Moses's interest in learning new things.
- ☐ E. It helps the reader know how the animals feel about Moses.

Directions: For questions 15 through 22, read *Just Call Them "Ginormous."* Then, answer the questions.

Just Call Them "Ginormous"

Adult African elephants are huge. Males can weigh as much as a school bus! Even their teeth are big—an adult's molar is the size of a brick. Their huge teeth help them grind and eat a lot of plant material every day. Our elephants at the Zoo and the Park each eat over 100 pounds of food each day.

At first glance, African elephants look similar to Asian elephants, but they are different species that live in different parts of the world. Here are some helpful clues for telling the two species apart: African elephants have very large ears that are shaped like the continent of Africa, while Asian elephants have smaller ears. Also, an Asian elephant's back is rounded, but an African elephant's back has a dip or sway in it. Their trunks are a little different, too: African elephants have two "fingers" at the end of their trunk, but Asian elephants have only one.

When most people think of elephants, they picture the large tusks. Both male and female African elephants have long tusks, which are actually teeth. Elephants dig with their tusks and use them to lift and move objects and to protect themselves. Sadly, people hunt elephants for these teeth. One reason these giants of the animal kingdom are threatened is because people want to collect their tusks.

15. There are many differences between African and Asian elephants.

Select **three** details from the passage that best support this idea.

☐ A. Their huge teeth help them grind and eat a lot of plant material every day.

☐ B. African elephants have two "fingers" at the end of their trunk, but Asian elephants have only one.

☐ C. They are different species that live in different parts of the world.

☐ D. Both African and Asian elephants have tusks that are actually teeth.

☐ E. African elephants have ears shaped like Africa, and Asian elephants have ears shaped like India.

☐ F. An Asian elephant's back is rounded, but an African elephant's back has a dip or sway in it.

16. The author uses a word that means to reduce (something) to small particles or powder by crushing it. Underline the word in the paragraph that is **closest** to that idea.

"Adult African elephants are huge. Males can weigh as much as a school bus! Even their teeth are big—an adult's molar is the size of a brick. Their huge teeth help them grind and eat a lot of plant material every day. Our elephants at the Zoo and the Park each eat over 100 pounds of food each day."

17. What inference can be made about why the author uses the word "ginormous" in the title? Support your answer with details from the passage.

----

18. What is the main idea of the following paragraph?

"At first glance, African elephants look similar to Asian elephants, but they are different species that live in different parts of the world. Here are some helpful clues for telling the two species apart: African elephants have very large ears that are shaped like the continent of Africa, while Asian elephants have smaller ears. Also, an Asian elephant's back is rounded, but an African elephant's back has a dip or sway in it. Their trunks are a little different, too: African elephants have two 'fingers' at the end of their trunk, but Asian elephants have only one."

----

19. Underline the sentence that gives the best conclusion about why the author includes information about tusks in the passage. Support your answer with details from the passage.

"When most people think of elephants, they picture the large tusks. Both male and female African elephants have long tusks, which are actually teeth. Elephants dig with their tusks and use them to lift and move objects and to protect themselves. Sadly, people hunt elephants for these teeth. One reason these giants of the animal kingdom are threatened is because people want to collect their tusks."

----

20. This question has two parts. Use your answer to Part A to answer the question in Part B.

Part A. Choose the sentence that **best** describes the author's point of view.

- O   A.   The author believes that only African elephants' tusks should be protected.
- O   B.   The author believes that African elephants are huge but should be protected from those who only want their tusks.
- O   C.   The author believes that Asian elephants are rather small, compared to African elephants.
- O   D.   The author believes that all elephants should eat over 100 pounds of food a day.

Part B. Which **two** sentences from the passage **best** support your answer to Part A?

- ☐   A.   "One reason these giants of the animal kingdom are threatened is because people want to collect their tusks."
- ☐   B.   "Males can weigh as much as a school bus!"
- ☐   C.   "African elephants have very large ears that are shaped like the continent of Africa, while Asian elephants have smaller ears."
- ☐   D.   "Even their teeth are big—an adult's molar is the size of a brick."
- ☐   E.   "Adult African elephants are huge."
- ☐   F.   "When most people think of elephants, they picture the large tusks."

21. What is the **most likely** reason the author used an exclamation point after the word "bus?"

- O   A.   To show different forms of punctuation
- O   B.   To compare African elephants' size to something we see every day
- O   C.   To show how a school bus is like an elephant tusk
- O   D.   To make the reader think about school

22. Put a check mark in the box that shows how African elephants are different from Asian elephants.

	Just African Elephants	Both	Just Asian Elephants
May have tusks			
Have a trunk with two "fingers"			
Have a rounded back			

Directions: A student is writing an opinion paper for class about why people should conserve energy. Read the draft of the essay, and answer questions 23 through 28.

Conservation

by I. Noah Student

We can save the earth by doing many things. It is important to save the earth because the earth is getting warmer because we are polluting the air!

One thing we can do is shut off the lights because some people do not shut off the lights, and once someone does it, the whole world will <u>do</u> it.

Another thing to save the earth is to not pollute the air because we need fresh air to breath. Same with animals, they need clean air, too. So that means we do not use cars as much because we can walk, bike, run and again once someone does it, then the whole world does. Plus we can walk, bike, run we can do all those things at home or go out to the playground.

We should not throw garbage out the window because that would be litering. Do not throw trash in the recycling. Use the recycling bins that your town provides for you. Recycling what you can is the best, so that we can use things again.

Also the trees give us air, or oxygen. People need to plant more trees so we have more air. We should not cut down trees because trees give us oxygen. You should only cut down trees if you replant trees. Trees can also save money because if you plant a tree that has food, then that is how you save your money since you can eat what you plant.

23. The beginning of the essay does not state the author's opinion. Rewrite the opening paragraph so it states the opinion and explains what the paper is about.

----

24. The writer wants to replace the <u>underlined</u> word in paragraph 2 to make her meaning clearer. Which **two** words would make her word choice **better**?

☐ A. Stop
☐ B. Conserve
☐ C. Follow
☐ D. Go
☐ E. Shut off
☐ F. Turn on

25. Choose the sentence that has a spelling error.

○ A. We should not throw garbage out the window because that would be litering.
○ B. Do not throw trash in the recycling.
○ C. Use the recycling bins that your town provides for you.
○ D. Recycling what you can is the best, so that we can use things again.

26. Which of the following sentences has an error in grammar usage?

○ A. We should not cut down trees because trees give us oxygen.
○ B. It is important to save the earth because the earth is getting warmer because we are polluting the air!
○ C. You can also save money if you plant a tree that has food, because you can eat what you plant.
○ D. People need to plant more trees so we can have more oxygen.

27. Which statement **best** describes how we can conserve energy to save the planet?

    O A.   Another thing to save the earth is to not pollute the air with car exhaust because we need fresh air to breath.

    O B.   Same with animals, they need clean air, too.

    O C.   So that means we do not use cars as much because we can walk, bike, and run to places.

    O D.   Once someone starts conserving, then the whole world does.

28. Choose a transitional phrase that would better start the paragraph below:

"We should not throw garbage out the window because that would be littering. Do not throw trash in the recycling. Use the recycling bins that your town provides for you. Recycling what you can is the best, so that we can use things again."

    O A.   Another thing

    O B.   There's another reason

    O C.   Finally,

    O D.   In addition to not polluting the air,

English Language Arts Answers Explained

Chapter 3: Responding in Full Sentences and Answering the Question Asked

Sample Responses for Practice Questions (pages 22–25)

The following responses are leveled to show a range of responses and bolded with the TTQA (Turn the Question Around) to show its effectiveness in writing responses to text.

1. What important bodily function is *sighing* linked to?

   Too brief response: Breathing.

   Lacking details response: Sighing is linked to breathing.

   Detailed response: ***The important bodily function that is linked to sighing*** is breathing a full breath, reaching down to the bottom of the lungs. The article says that most people, when breathing, do not actually take a full breath. Sighing helps people take even more air into their lungs, so that more oxygen is flowing with the breath.

2. **Part A: (B)** Alveoli are tiny sacs in the lungs.

   Part B. Based on your answer to Part A, describe about how many alveoli are present in your lungs, and what they are able to do for your lungs.

   Too brief response: Tiny sacs.

   Lacking details response: Alveoli are tiny sacs in the lungs.

   Detailed response: ***Alveoli are actually millions of tiny sacs in the lungs that*** "inflate and collapse as we breathe in and out." (paragraph 3) The alveoli are also the places in our lungs where oxygen and carbon dioxide are exchanged. This is important because we need oxygen to breathe. In the passage, it also mentions that the alveoli are the places where the circulatory system connects with the respiratory system. Such tiny places have important jobs in our lungs.

3. How is sadness connected to sighing and breathing?

   Too brief response: Sighing is sad.

   Lacking details response: Because it makes you take a deeper breath when you're sad.

   Detailed response: *Sadness is connected to sighing and breathing because* when people sigh, they are actually taking a deeper breath. Sometimes when people are sad, they feel the need to sigh. So, when you sigh from sadness, you are actually helping your lungs function better because taking a deeper, a sighing breath, inflates the tiny sacs, or alveoli, in your lungs, which increases the oxygen intake in each breath. The passage also mentions that you don't have to be sad to sigh, but often people are sad when they sigh.

4. Why is the connection between the lungs and brain so important during sighing?

   Too brief response: Your brain knows it.

   Lacking details response: When you breathe, you take in air and your brain knows that you're breathing.

   Detailed response: *The connection between your brain and your lungs during sighing is important because* there are these peptides, which are little proteins your brain needs to know about, that are increased when you take a big breath. The peptides send messages to your brain cells and that helps your lungs function better. Most people need to sigh in order to take a big enough breath for the alveoli to be inflated completely, which then fill the whole lungs with air.

5. Explain why this discovery could be important in respiratory science.

   Too brief response: Sighing is cool.

   Lacking details response: Because we have more air to breathe in when we sigh.

   Detailed response: *Sighing is an important discovery in respiratory science because* it turns out to be an incredibly important, life-saving involuntary response. In order for the alveoli in our lungs to properly inflate, they need to have some air in them, and then even a bit more in order to be inflated completely. When this happens, the lungs are able to properly make the exchange of oxygen and carbon dioxide from the circulatory system. This is what keeps us alive.

Chapter 4: Incorporating Text in Written Responses

Sample Responses for Practice Questions with Annotation (pages 28–34)

1. I know the genre of this text is fiction for several reasons. First, an elephant falls from out of nowhere. It says in the text, "the elephant that came through the roof." Elephants do not just fall through a roof. Second, the elephant came because of a magician. The text says, "the elephant conjured by the magician," which means that if the elephant happened by magic, it may not be real. Finally, it says that fortune tellers were busy, and that "If elephants could arrive without warning, then a dramatic shift had certainly occurred in the universe." It seems no one knew the elephant was coming, and now even the fortune tellers are working hard to figure things out. Not everyone believes in fortune tellers, but they could be real. So, this text is fiction because the details about an elephant just appearing may not be real.

   Note: Many students will respond simply, "The genre is fiction because elephants falling from the sky isn't real." Using transition words like first, second, third and finally, all will help your child organize information and remind him to answer the question fully. Always remind your child to write/type in full sentences.

2. This particular question is difficult to simulate on paper, but you need to realize that portions of each sentence will be active for your child to "click on." For this particular question, I would have underlined "the people could not get enough of it." And, "The elephant's dramatic and unexpected appearance changed the way the people of the city of Baltese spoke." Both of these sentences support the assertion that the people of Baltese were in awe of the elephant.

3. **Part A: D** The central idea of the passage is "The elephant has taken all the attention in the city of Baltese, and the Countess does not like that."

   Part B: C To support your answer to Part A, you should choose, "I truly feel, I am quite certain, I am absolutely convinced, that I will lose my mind if I hear the word *elephant* one more time."

   In Part B, the statement supports the notion that the Countess does not want this elephant around because it is stealing all the attention from her.

4. **B** Exorbitant means very expensive. Context clues for this word would be the parts that hint at cost, namely, "the street vendors sold" and "price."

5. The correct order of these events is as follows:

An elephant fell through a roof unexpectedly. People began talking about an elephant that seemed magical. The children laughed at puppets who re-enacted the appearance of the elephant. A new phrase came into being that meant one was as surprised as when the elephant arrived in the city of Baltese. The fortune tellers made new predictions with their tea leaves.

I positioned the events in paragraph form. When third graders are asked similar questions about putting events of the story in order, the computer tools will let them drag and relocate the events, but the events will pop into place to form a paragraph.

6. The inference I can make about what is important to the people of Baltese is that they really like elephants all of the sudden. The text supports this because it says that they "became obsessed with the elephant." Also, the people of Baltese have puppet shows about the elephant, which make "the young children laugh and clap in delight and recognition." The Baltese people even start changing how they speak. The text says, "If, for instance, a person was deeply surprised or moved, he or she would say, "I was, you understand, in the presence of the elephant." They make a new food about the elephant, and call it "elephant ears," and it's a sweet pastry for all to eat. Finally, the Countess of Baltese says, "It is all people will speak of." Everyone in Baltese, from children to the Countess are talking about the elephant.

7. The author's message in sharing this passage is that she would like to show the reader that a whole city of people get excited about something extraordinary together. In Baltese, this extraordinary thing happens because an elephant falls out of the sky. This elephant's appearance is so unusual that the whole city focuses only on elephants. It seems to bring excitement in the community to everyone but the Countess Quintet. From puppet shows for children, to how people speak, to making elephant ears, to how the Count and Countess react, everyone is excited about the elephants. Even the fortune tellers of the city are busy, and the people of Baltese may wonder what else extraordinary will happen to them.

8. This question is different for third graders because it asks them to click on three reasons that support the assertion. Including dialogue in the passage is useful because:

A It helps the reader understand that the people of the city of Baltese are dramatic.

E It helps the reader understand how the people of the city of Baltese believed the fortune tellers.

F It helps the reader understand why the bakers made the elephant ear.

This type of question also forces your child to think specifically about answering a question with support that they may or may not agree with. The question doesn't ask their opinion, it asks what statements support the assertion. This is tough for third graders because they often want to argue with the text, and then may be frustrated that the things they think are not the reasons are the choices they have to choose from.

9. **D** The phrase about the Countess tells the reader that, "The Countess puts a lot of stock in appearances and social status."

   Even if your child does not fully comprehend what a "social season" is, he or she is probably familiar with the word social. Helping your child use what he or she already knows is key to decreasing stress and increasing focus on responding to the test questions.

10. Answers will vary with creativity, but should include taking the Count's advice, or totally rejecting his advice. Children could go on to continue to create elephant craziness along with the people of Baltese. Since so much credence is given to the fortune tellers, the story may include something else revealing about a fortune.

Chapter 5: Reading for Purpose: Analyzing Poetry

Answers and Suggested Responses for Practice Questions (pages 37–39)

1. **B** *Equi-* is a prefix meaning equal. Distance is a length of time.

2. **D** The tone of the poem is bleak, and conjures many images of loneliness— bare trees, gray, wondering, dismal, heartbreak—all are words that make one feel lonely.

3. **A, C** The repetition of a villanelle highlights the main theme of the poem. In a villanelle, there are specific lines that repeat for emphasis to assist the reader's understanding of what the poet is thinking. In this case, the repeating lines, "Driving gray lanes equidistant to you" and "Imagining bare trees my band and crew," both reveal a sense of a long drive where one might not reach the other, but will be separated, and even watched by others. That's pretty lonely.

4. **C** The average reader does not need to know that the exact rhyme scheme of a villanelle is ABA, ABA, ABA, ABA, ABA, ABAA. However, one can look at the last words of each line and note which words rhyme and in what order.

5. **D** Given the other words in the poem: bare trees, dismal, gray skies, high clouds, all of which exhibit a cold, wintry feeling, a point could be made that while the speaker is probably in a car, he or she is not referring to parts of the car, but a frozen lake. Also, ice is often compared to glass, which is a connection children could make on their own.

6. Suggested response:

Wishes could be compared to rock slides in a couple ways. First, sometimes you wish for something, and it just stays stuck, like a big rock going nowhere. It's steep because it doesn't feel like you can reach it, and it never moves, so it cannot shake. Second, wishes can be like rock slides because they could tumble right down and make you feel crushed, like the wish never happened, or you wished for the wrong thing. In that case, the rock slide would shake because your wish didn't happen.

7. Suggested response:

Two characteristics of driving are that it takes a long time, and you have plenty of time to look out the window and see the trees. I know this because the poet repeats "Driving gray lanes equidistant to you" and "Imagining bare trees my band and crew," both of which make me think of long, parallel lines on a long trip and staring out the window seeing a lot of trees on the side of the road. Also, you can listen to music when you're driving, and that can help the drive go faster, or just help when you're in the car and imagining the music with you in the car.

8. Suggested Response:

The "band and crew" could be the people driving in the car. Even though the poem infers it's a lonely drive, there could be other people in the car listening to music and not talking to one another. They could be singing to the music. Also, the band and crew could actually be the bare trees, as they stand tall like a crew helping out the band and supporting them in their musical travels.

9. Suggested Response:

The season this poem probably takes place in is the winter. In lines 7 and 8 it says, "Slender branches reach up to gray sky clues" and "Melodic memories sit like a glass lake." Also, in line 4 it says, "Winter always wonders at what is true." I think all three of these lines show that the season is winter, when trees are bare, skies are gray, and lakes are frozen.

Chapter 6: English Language Arts Practice Test (pages 41–55)

1. "After talking with my mom, she just smirked at me, gave me a hug, and said, 'Sure, honey, you can bring your pet mouse with you, as long as he wears his scrubs in the hospitals.'

   I called him the next day. He was coming with us. I couldn't wait to have such an informative traveling companion."

   The underlined sentence shows that the narrator's mom understands her child is using his imagination because she smirks. Usually when people smirk they are suggesting a double meaning. The mom knows her child has some worries about traveling to Uganda, but she also knows that using one's imagination can always help for the better. Perhaps the child has used his imagination before to find comfort.

2. **B and D** These are the only two choices that show the boy has some worries about traveling to Africa. Choice A suggests that the mom will not believe her son, as he wants to bring a mouse with him to a hospital in Uganda. Choice B reveals that if the mom accepts he's bringing the mouse (even though it's imaginary), then he also knows that mice aren't accepted visitors of a human hospital.

3. Suggested response.

   The conclusion that can be drawn from the author's point of view is that the author believes that the boy can use his imagination to get through a difficult trip. Moses loves his mom, but he is a little leery of going so far away to a place he's never been to with people he may not understand. The reader can tell he loves his mom because in the passage it says they go everywhere together. Also, it seems he goes to the zoo to gather information, or make himself feel more comfortable about traveling to a place he perceives to be so foreign to him, which in itself relies on using one's imagination.

This is a difficult question. The reader needs to infer that the boy is using his imagination and explain how using his imagination comforts him while traveling. It is clear the mother loves her son, and finds it meaningful for him to travel with her when she travels around the world as a doctor.

4. **C and D** The paragraph chosen is the first paragraph of the passage. It indeed sets up the characters as mother and son, and gives ample hints that the mom is probably a doctor.

5. **D** A common usage of the word "piqued" is to "pique one's curiosity." While all responses may be true to the story, the only response that indicates a sense of kindling excitement or curiosity is choice D.

6. **B** This choice shows how the author used onomatopoeia, using words to exhibit the actual sounds they make, to show how an antelope might sound while talking with its mouth full. Also, squarsh is a made-up word, which would further signify a playfulness with language.

7. Suggested response.

> I can infer that the narrator of this story is an imaginative boy for several reasons. He chooses to visit a zoo to get information from actual African animals before he travels to Africa. As a reader, we need to make that leap into fiction, or accept the idea of suspension of disbelief to believe that Moses is actually talking with animals. Also, the reader probably finds Moses and his talking animal companions likable, so it is easier to believe that he could be talking to animals. I believe that Moses is an actual human because, even if he is also a made-up character, a real boy could have a mom who is a doctor, and they could be traveling all over the world to care for the sick. Also, the details like the Portland Zoo and Uganda all show actual details that are true. Using real facts helps make the story come alive, as well as make it more believable that Moses could actually be talking to animals, even if they're in his imagination.

Whenever children travel, they may feel some trepidation about the unknown, even if they are used to traveling. The coping device Moses seems to be using is his active imagination. It is believable that a young, intelligent boy would use his imagination to make the traveling both more fun and more comfortable.

8. **D** Of course, students need to remember that the word "synonym" means a word very similar in meaning to another word. Choice D is correct because it matches up the synonyms with each of the words underlined in the text. This type of question invites students to use the process of elimination and encourages them to slow down and organize their thoughts, as the other choices are closely aligned to the synonyms.

9. I just couldn't believe I was talking to an elephant. "Oh wow," I said to myself.

   The seven errors are corrected:

   1. coldnt should be couldn't

   2. beleive should be believe

   3. a should be an (before a noun which begins with a vowel)

   4. elefant should be elephant

   5. and 6. Oh wow should be "Oh wow," (dialogue should be between quotation marks and beset with a comma)

   7. There should be a period at the end of the sentence.

10. **Part A: B, Part B: C** The narrator of the story is an imaginative and intelligent boy. Even if it is true that he visited the Portland Zoo, he uses his imagination to create characters to help him come to terms with the exciting adventures he's about to partake. He is going to a foreign land with different people, and using the mouse as a "tour guide" may help him mitigate all this newness.

11. **A and C** While all the choices are details from the story, only choices A and C are details that support why Musapo the Mouse would be the best animal tour guide Moses could bring with him to Uganda.

12. Suggested response.

    The author mentions Musapo's religion to show that people in different countries may have different beliefs from Moses, or people traveling anywhere within or beyond the borders of one's country. In Musapo's discussion with Moses, the author explains that Musapo reassures Moses that no matter what religion someone practices, all people can find common ground. The author also seems to suggest that Moses's mom is a doctor, and it is a doctor's duty to attend to all people, no matter their religion.

Many times students read a story and may not realize the lessons within it. While this story is imaginative, it also shows that being different and adventurous can be a good thing, just as staying at home can be comforting as well. The animals and the narrator show they care about differences and learning about them. Also, the SBAC is an assessment that reaches all aspects of our culture. It is possible students will need to have an open mind to learning about new views while taking the test.

13. The correct order is

    1. Moses visits the Portland Zoo to do some research.

    2. Elvira tells Moses that she doesn't remember much about her homeland.

    3. Aeneas answers Moses's questions while talking with her mouth full.

    4. Musapo meets Moses and decides to go with him on his trip to Uganda.

    5. Moses's mom tells him it's okay to bring Musapo with him to Uganda.

14. **A, C, and D** These three choices are correct because Moses tells the animals why he is asking them questions about Uganda, and that he is going to Uganda. When Moses tells his mom he would like to bring Musapo the mouse to Uganda with him, it shows that his mom loves him because she hugs him, smirks at him, and playfully tells him to be careful with the mouse while they are in the hospital. And finally, we learn Moses has an interest in learning new things when he talks with the animals. His conversations show us what he is thinking about before leaving to go on this great adventure.

15. **B, C, and F** These three responses are taken directly from the text to show the differences between African and Asian elephants. The other choices are facts, but they do not exemplify the **differences** between the two species of elephants.

16. Adult African elephants are huge. Males can weigh as much as a school bus! Even their teeth are big—an adult's molar is the size of a brick. Their huge teeth help them <u>grind</u> and eat a lot of plant material every day. Our elephants at the Zoo and the Park each eat over 100 pounds of food each day.

    The definition of grind is to crush something into smaller pieces.

17. Suggested response.

> The inference that can be made about why the author uses the word "ginormous" in the title is to show how enormous elephants are. Ginormous is also a more descriptive word than huge.

The word "ginormous" is a more informal, playful, and specific way to say huge, and may invite the readers into the story, especially since the passage was from an online elephant description at the San Diego Zoo, a place where children could visit and read at their level.

18. Suggested response.

> The main idea of this paragraph is to compare the differences between African and Asian elephants. Most people may not know that African and Asian elephants are actually considered two different species, and this paragraph shows some of the differences between the two. It is helpful to know these differences are evident by just looking at an elephant.

The topic sentence of the paragraph clearly states the main idea: "At first glance, African elephants look similar to Asian elephants, but they are different species that live in different parts of the world." The paragraph then goes on to show three differences—the ears, the back, and the trunk.

19. When most people think of elephants, they picture the large tusks. Both male and female African elephants have long tusks, which are actually teeth. Elephants dig with their tusks and use them to lift and move objects and to protect themselves. <u>Sadly, people hunt elephants for these teeth.</u> One reason these giants of the animal kingdom are threatened is because people want to collect their tusks.

Suggested response.

> I chose the sentence "Sadly, people hunt elephants for these teeth" because it shows that it is really sad that people kill elephants just for their tusks. The beginning of the paragraph tells how elephants use their tusks to dig, lift things, and protect themselves. Without their tusks they cannot do that. If people did not hunt elephants for their tusks, then the last sentence of the paragraph wouldn't happen. Elephants would not be threatened if people didn't want their tusks so much.

The assertion that "Sadly, people hunt elephants for these teeth" shows the reader that the author believes it is sad that people are killing elephants for just their tusks. The sample response shows that the student has a thorough understanding about this assertion as being a very real statement about why protecting elephants, these "giants of the animal kingdom," is so important.

20. **Part A: B, Part B: A and E** Choices A and E in Part B are evidence in the text to support the assertion in Part A, choice B. While the other choices in Part B are indeed facts, they do not support the author's point of view that these "ginormous" creatures should be protected from those who want them only for their tusks.

21. **B** Because children readily know how large a school bus is, it is reasonable to compare an elephant's size to one. The exclamation point sets off the comparison to show just how large elephants are in reality.

22.

	Just African Elephants	Both	Just Asian Elephants
May have tusks		✔	
Have a trunk with two "fingers"	✔		
Have a rounded back			✔

The passage does not mention if either type of elephant lacks tusks, so it is safe to conclude that both species of elephants may have trunks. Also, the passage clearly states that African elephants have trunks with two "fingers" at the bottom, so as to grab food. And finally, the second paragraph reveals that the Asian elephants have rounded backs, and the African elephants have a dip or sway in their backs.

23. Suggested response.

We can save the earth by doing many things. I believe that conservation is helpful to think about saving our planet in four ways. I think everyone could use less electricity, drive cars less, recycle more trash, and plant more trees. By doing these simple things, more people could contribute to keeping our earth healthy.

This sample student response shows a clearly stated opinion: "I believe that conservation is helpful to think about saving our planet in four ways." The reader can then see in a very organized manner that the next four paragraphs will show which four ways the writer would like to showcase for others to consider conserving more.

24. **B and C** Both the words "conserve" and "follow" would make sense in the sentence. The writer wrote "do," but it is not exactly clear what the reader should "do."

25. **A** Littering is missing a "t" in the item response.

26. **B** This sentence has "because" twice. It is not considered correct grammar usage to include the word "because" more than once in one sentence. When stating a clear cause and effect, a writer should only use the word because one time per sentence. Also, the first part of the sentence, "It is important to save the earth," could be a sentence within itself. The second two parts of the sentence would make more sense if written like this: "The earth is getting warmer because we are polluting the air."

27. **A** This choice is correct because that is the only response that offers a clear connection between what a person can do to help conserve energy and save the planet.

28. **D** This choice is correct because it connects the previous paragraph in the draft to the paragraph that begins. The student already uses "another" in an earlier paragraph, so using it again would be repetitive. "Finally" would be a poor transition word occurring in a middle paragraph.

PART TWO
Math

What Every 3rd Grader Needs to Know About the Smarter Balanced Grade 3 Math Exam

This section of the book is designed to help your child understand third-grade math and prepare him or her for the Smarter Balanced Assessments. By working through this book, your child will get an in-depth understanding of the third-grade Common Core standards. In third grade, your child is expected to understand the following math topics: Operations and Algebraic Thinking, Number and Operations in Base 10, Number and Operations—Fractions, Measurement and Data, and Geometry. Your child will be expected to demonstrate the following knowledge in each of these topics:

Operations and Algebraic Thinking

> Represent and solve problems using multiplication and division

> Understand properties of multiplication and the relationship between multiplying and dividing

> Multiply and divide within 100

> Solve problems involving addition, subtraction, multiplication, and division. In addition, identify and explain patterns in arithmetic

Number and Operations in Base 10

> Use place value understanding and the properties of operations to perform multi-digit math problems

Number and Operations—Fractions

> Develop understanding of fractions as numbers

Measurement and Data

> Solve problems involving measurement and estimation

> Represent and interpret data

> Geometric measurement: Understand concepts of area and relate area to multiplication and to addition

> Geometric measurement: Recognize perimeter

Geometry

> Reason with shapes and their attributes

The Common Core Standards are organized as learning progressions across different grades. This means that what your child learns in each grade level builds on each other. The Common Core Standards outline what math your child should **understand** and what he or she should be **able to do**. For example, your child should learn the multiplication facts. However, if he or she only memorizes the facts such as $5 \times 5 = 25$, he or she may not understand why 5×5 is 25 and what that means. If it is understood that 5×5 means you are adding five groups of five things, then this knowledge can be used to help solve other problems he or she doesn't know. Therefore, understanding math is not just about memorizing rules, but figuring out why the rule works. When math makes sense, children are able to use it to solve problems in real-world situations. Understanding math and being a good student involves:

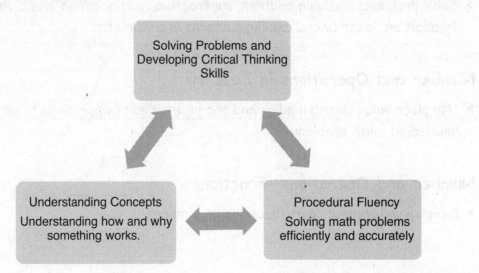

What Are the Smarter Balanced Assessments?

The Smarter Balanced Assessments are tests that are taken on the computer. You and your child can find more information about the online test and become familiar with the format by visiting the following website:

http://www.smarterbalanced.org/assessments/practice-and-training-tests/

At this website, your child can take an online practice test. Make sure to select the third-grade practice test. This will help familiarize your child with the computerized format. The question types used in the online practice test have been used as a model for the types of test questions outlined in this book. This book will give your child more opportunities to practice similar test questions and also learn about the math behind these questions. Furthermore, by taking the online practice exam, your child will become familiar with the click and drag tools on the computer and will be able to practice questions where he or she will have to type answers in a box.

How to Use This Book

Students

Use this book as a resource to study for the Smarter Balanced Test. The best way to prepare is to manage your time. Break the sections into smaller chunks and do one section at a time. Read the "Big Idea" section and then do the practice problems that follow. The best way to use this book is in conjunction with the topics you are learning at school. For example, when you are learning about fractions at school, you can work on the fraction section in this book. Math topics are explained briefly at the beginning of each chapter. Then, practice problems and explanations are provided to make sure you understand the key ideas discussed. At the end of each chapter is a chapter review on the topic. Each chapter includes a progress checklist to help you keep track of your progress. Chapter 14 contains a Math practice test.

Teachers

This book is a great resource for you to use in conjunction with your grade-level curriculum. The Common Core math domains are outlined for you along with the key ideas that students should learn. This can help drive your teaching to ensure that students understand the math conceptually and procedurally. These key ideas are based on the standards and research in mathematics education. The standards have been made easily accessible for you to understand the "big picture" of what students should learn in each domain as well as the skills they need to develop. Each content chapter provides a checklist of concepts that students should understand. Create a class checklist and keep track of what students should know. The key ideas are listed in the rubric. Examples of assessment rubrics created by teachers can be found in the following blog:

http://www.mathdiscussions.wordpress.com

Each content chapter provides sample problem types that students should be familiar with. Integrate these problem types into your regular lessons. You can choose problems from this book to pose to students as a warm up. You can also use problems from this book as an assessment of student learning.

Parents

Use this book as a resource to support your child to be successful in the Smarter Balanced Assessments and Common Core topics by providing support at home. Each chapter includes a brief summary of the "key ideas" with sample problem types. There is too much information to learn at once. Therefore, help your child break down the standards into manageable chunks. It is recommended that you use this book as a supplement to your child's instruction at school. When your child is learning a particular topic, encourage him or her to read the corresponding chapter and solve the sample problems in this book. Break down the sections into manageable chunks. Let your child experience success and then build on it. If your child does not understand a particular problem, have him or her re-read the section on the key ideas and then try the problem again.

Standards for Mathematical Practice

The Standards for Mathematical Practice are guidelines developed to help your child develop problem solving and critical thinking skills. Jobs of the future and today require you to be able to think through problems, come up with solutions, and communicate your thinking to others.

The Standards for Mathematical Practice in the Common Core Standards outline a process that helps you develop problem solving and thinking skills. There are eight math practices that you should be following when learning math. These practices help you develop the abilities that will make you a better math student. Math becomes hard when you only memorize a bunch of steps and formulas. When you just memorize things without understanding what you are doing, math does not make sense. However, when you try to make sense of math and understand what you are doing, math becomes more meaningful and fun. When you solve math problems, you should be using the math practices. This does not mean that you have to use all the practices at once. Instead, know what they are, and determine which ones to use for a particular problem. The practices are described below. An example problem is provided to show you how the math practices can be used to solve problems.

Example Problem

Mr. Moss's class is going to the science museum. The cost of the trip is $150 for 25 kids. The class made $100 at the bake sale. How much more money do they need to go on the trip? How much does each ticket cost?

1. **Make sense of problems and persevere in solving them.**

   - Figure out what the problem is asking you to do? Think about the information given and what you need to do to get started.
   - Come up with a plan to solve the problem, try things out.
   - See if your answers make sense.
   - Keep working, don't give up!

   Read the problem and organize your information. What information is given, and what is the problem asking you to do?

   Information given: Mr. Moss's class is going to the Science Museum.

   There are 25 kids going on the field trip. The total cost for the 25 kids is $150.

   $100 was raised at the bake sale.

   The problem is asking you to:

   - Figure out how much more money is needed. You already have $100, and you need $150.
   - You need to figure out how much each ticket costs?

   This problem requires more than one step, so it is easy to break it into manageable chucks. You can work on one part at a time.

STEP 1 Figure out how much money is needed. Make a plan. You already know that you have $100, and that you need $150. You can set up a subtraction problem:

$$\$150 - 100 = ?$$

You can also think about it as an addition problem. You can add 100 +? = $150.

There are many ways the problem can be solved. Figure out a strategy that makes sense to you.

STEP 2 The second part of the problem involves figuring out how much each ticket costs. You already know the total is $150, and you also know that there are 25 kids. This is a division problem. You can set up the problem as 150 ÷ 25 to figure out the answer.

- Come up with a plan to solve the problem, try things out.
- See if your answers make sense.
- Keep working, don't give up!

2. **Reason abstractly and quantitatively.**

- Use pictures and models to think about the problem.
- Use number sentences and math symbols to represent the math problem.

Example

You can use pictures or manipulatives to think about the problem of how much more money is needed. You can then represent your model using numbers.

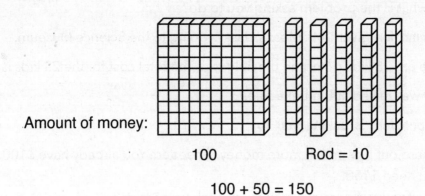

Amount of money:

100   Rod = 10

100 + 50 = 150

3. **Construct viable arguments and critique the reasoning of others.**

- You should be able to explain your thinking to justify your answer.
- You should be able to evaluate another person's answer to see if it makes sense. Do you agree or disagree with that person's point of view?

Example

You should be able to explain how you got your answer and defend it. For example, you can explain how you counted to get $150 by saying, "I started with the 100 block, and then I added five 10 rods, which made 50. So I got $150. "

Suppose a classmate said, "I got $175 because I added $150 and $25." For example, you could point out that this does not make sense because 25 represents the number of kids who went on the field trip and not the money. So, it does not make sense to add the numbers up.

4. **Model with mathematics.**

- Use math to solve real-world problems.
- Model real-world situations using math.

Example

Number of kids	Number of kids going on the field trip = 25	Cost per kids $150 ÷ 25 = $6
Cost for 25 kids		$100 + $50 = $150 Money needed for the field trip
		$100—The amount of money the class has for the field trip. To figure out the money needed for the field trip, the following equation can be solved: $100 + ? = $150

5. **Use appropriate tools strategically.**

   - Figure out which tools to use to solve math problems.

   Example

   This problem can be solved using a calculator or manipulatives, such as place value blocks, play money, or scratch paper. Use a tool that makes sense and makes it easy for you to solve the problem.

6. **Attend to precision.**

   - Use accurate math vocabulary to describe a situation.
   - Make sure the problems are mathematically accurate.

   When figuring out how much money is needed, you can either use addition or subtraction. Make sure you point out the values that are dollars.

   Example

   You can figure out the correct amount by using addition.

   $$\$100 + ? = \$150$$

   Or you can use subtraction.

   $$\$150 - \$100 = \$50$$

   By using accurate vocabulary to describe what you are doing and also pointing out what the numbers mean, such as dollars, you are using precise vocabulary and solving the problem.

7. **Look for and make use of structure.**

   - Look for patterns when solving problems and figure out the easiest way to solve the problem.

   Example

   You may see the connection between multiplying and dividing. You can see that $25 \times 6 = 150$ is similar to figuring out the problem using the division problem $150 \div 25 = 6$.

8. **Look for and express regularity in repeated reasoning.**

- Think about the big mathematical ideas when solving problems.
- Look for patterns.

Example

You can notice patterns in calculations.

For example, you may notice that whenever you divide, you are doing repeated subtraction.

$150 \div 25$ involves subtracting a group of 25 from the whole of 150.

Operations and Algebraic Thinking

Multiplication

When multiplying, you are adding the same number many times. In order to do this, you need to know the number of groups and the size of each group. The two numbers that you multiply together are called **factors**. The answer is called the **product**.

For example, think about the following problem.

There are 4 children. Each child gets 3 cookies. How many cookies are there in all?

The number of groups	The size of group
4 (children)	3 (Each child gets 3 cookies.)

We know the size of the group of cookies that each child gets is 3. There are 4 children. We can think about this multiplication problem as the total of 4 groups of 3 cookies. We can write this as an addition sentence 3 + 3 + 3 + 3, but it is easier to write this using the multiplication sentence 4 × 3.

Once you understand how to multiply, you may just remember that $4 \times 3 = 12$. If you remember that multiplication involves adding a group of items multiple times, you can use this information to figure out any multiplication fact that you don't remember. There are many ways to figure out how to multiply. Keep working on trying to figure out more efficient ways to solve problems. At some point, you will need to memorize multiplication facts so that you can do more complex problems later on. When you understand how multiplication works, you will have an easier time solving multiplication problems.

Suppose you were given the multiplication problem 3×4. There are several ways to solve this problem. You can use equal sets, where you add a number multiple times using counters, you can draw a picture, you can create an array, or you can figure it out on a number line.

Equal Sets

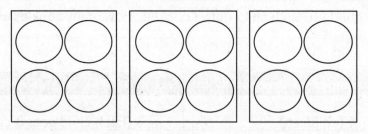

$$4 + 4 + 4$$

Array

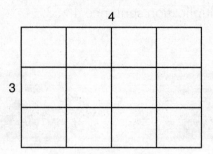

Number line

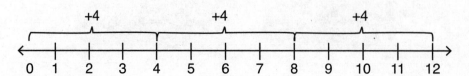

Multiplication Properties

The following rules (properties of multiplication) work every time when solving multiplication problems. Knowing these rules will help you learn your multiplication facts and find easier ways to multiply.

Commutative Property of Multiplication

The order of the numbers that you multiply does not matter. You will still get the same product.

Note: The product is the answer to a multiplication problem.

Example

$3 \times 5 = 15$ is the same as $5 \times 3 = 15$

Multiplying 3 groups of 5 will give you the same answer as multiplying 5 groups of 3.

Associative Property of Multiplication

When you are multiplying 3 or more numbers, you can multiply the numbers in any order, and you will get the same product.

Example

$2 \times 6 \times 3$ can be found by multiplying $2 \times 6 = 12$, then multiplying $12 \times 3 = 36$, or by multiplying $6 \times 3 = 18$, and then multiplying $18 \times 2 = 36$.

Distributive Property

You can split the factors into smaller parts and then multiply them.

Example

You can figure out $7 \times 8 = 56$ by using friendlier numbers. So, you can think about it as: $7 \times 8 = (7 \times 5) + (7 \times 3)$

$$(7 \times 5) + (7 \times 3)$$
$$35 \quad + \quad 21 = 56$$

TIPS FOR LEARNING MULTIPLICATION

> Look for patterns in the multiplication table. What patterns do you notice?

> Use what you know to solve problems. For example, think about the problem 3×5. You may already know that 2 times 5 is 10. So, you only have to add 5 more to get 15.

> Figure out faster or more efficient ways to solve problems.

Here are some ways you can use to figure out the multiplication tables. You may come up with other ways. Explore patterns in the multiplication table to help you learn your multiplication facts. Remember, it is easier to learn your facts if you understand how multiplication works. This way, if you forget a fact, you can figure it out using different strategies.

Multiplication Table

×	1	2	3	4	5	6	7	8	9	10	11	12
1	1	2	3	4	5	6	7	8	9	10	11	12
2	2	4	6	8	10	12	14	16	18	20	22	24
3	3	6	9	12	15	18	21	24	27	30	33	36
4	4	8	12	16	20	24	28	32	36	40	44	48
5	5	10	15	20	25	30	35	40	45	50	55	60
6	6	12	18	24	30	36	42	48	54	60	66	72
7	7	14	21	28	35	42	49	56	63	70	77	84
8	8	16	24	32	40	48	56	64	72	80	88	96
9	9	18	27	36	45	54	63	72	81	90	99	108
10	10	20	30	40	50	60	70	80	90	100	110	120
11	11	22	33	44	55	66	77	88	99	110	121	132
12	12	24	36	48	60	72	84	96	108	120	132	144

Multiply	Strategies (different ways to solve problems)	Example
0	When you multiply any number by zero, the answer is always zero.	$2 \times 0 = 0$
1	When you multiply any number by 1, the answer remains the same.	$3 \times 1 = 3$
2	Double the number (add it twice).	$6 + 6 = 6 \times 2$ $6 \times 2 = 12$
3	Double number and add one more set of the number that you are doubling.	$2 \times 6 = 12$ $12 + 6 = 18$
4	You can double the number and double it again.	$8 \times 4 = (8 \times 2) + (8 \times 2)$ $16 + 16 = 32$
5	Multiply by 10 and divide by half.	**$5 \times 5 = 25$** You can half $5 \times 10 = 50$. Half of 50 is 25.
6	You can figure out what 3 times a number is and double it.	**$6 \times 4 = 24$** $3 \times 4 = 12$ If you double 12, you get 24.
7	You can think about a multiplication fact you know related to 7 and add the numbers up. For example, you may know 7×5 and 7×1. You can use this information to figure out 7×6.	**$7 \times 6 = 42$** $7 \times 5 = 35$ $7 \times 1 = 7$ $35 + 7 = 42$
8	Multiply a number by 4 and double it.	$8 \times 4 = 32$ $4 \times 4 = 16$. If you double 16, you get 32.
9	If you look at the 9s in the multiplication table, you may notice that the digits in the 10s and 1s place add up to 9. You may also notice that the answer in the 10s digit is one less than the number you are multiplying.	$9 \times 7 = 63$ Look at the multiplication table for 9s. Notice the digit in the 10s place is one less than 7 for 9×7. It is 6 in the 10s place. This means the digits in the 10s place and 1s place need to add up to 9. The digits $6 + 3 = 9$. The answer is 63.
10	If you multiply any number by 10, just add a zero to the number.	$7 \times 10 = 70$

Multiplication Practice Problems

(Answers can be found on pages 223–224.)

1. There are 3 dogs. Each dog eats 5 bones. How many bones do they eat in all? Which of the following represents this problem?

   O A. 3×5
   O B. 3×3
   O C. 5×5
   O D. 1×5

2. Keisha wants to buy 5 tickets to the movies. Each ticket costs $6. How much money does Keisha need to buy 5 tickets?

   O A. $6
   O B. $11
   O C. $30
   O D. $36

3. There are 6 children. Each child gets 3 cookies. How many total cookies did they share?

   O A. 18
   O B. 9
   O C. 11
   O D. 15

4. Penny has 5 notebooks. She puts 2 stickers on each notebook. How many stickers does Penny have in all? Which of the following represents this problem?

   O A. 5×1
   O B. 2×1
   O C. 5×2
   O D. 6×2

5. There are 7 boxes of chocolate. Each box contains 8 chocolate bars. What is the total amount of chocolate bars in all?

   O A. 15
   O B. 78
   O C. 54
   O D. 56

6. 9 × 3 = ?

    O A. 27

    O B. 25

    O C. 13

    O D. 12

7. 4 × 5 = ?

    O A. 14

    O B. 9

    O C. 20

    O D. 25

8. 8 × 3 = ?

    O A. 27

    O B. 23

    O C. 24

    O D. 12

9. 6 × 6 = ?

    O A. 36

    O B. 66

    O C. 12

    O D. 62

10. Which expression is equal to 4 × 7?

    O A. (2 × 7) + (2 × 7)

    O B. (4 × 5) + (4 × 2)

    O C. (7 × 4) + (7 × 4)

    O D. (4 × 3) + (7 × 3)

11. Marcy has 4 stacks of quarters. Jim has 9 stacks of quarters. Each stack of quarters is worth $2. How much more money, in dollars, does Jim have than Marcy?

   O A. $11

   O B. $13

   O C. $15

   O D. $10

12. The addition sentence 8 + 8 + 8 has the same value as which of the following?

   O A. $24 \div 8$

   O B. 3×8

   O C. $8 - 3$

   O D. $8 + 3$

13. Which array represents 2×8?

   O A.

   O B.

   O C.

   O D.

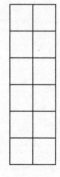

14. If you want to figure out 7 × 7, which equation can you use?

    ○ A. (7 × 3) + (2 × 7)
    ○ B. (7 × 7) + (7 × 7)
    ○ C. (7 + 2) + (7 − 5)
    ○ D. (7 × 2) + (7 × 5)

15. What unknown number completes the pattern on the number line?

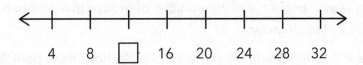

    4   8   □   16   20   24   28   32

    ○ A. 30
    ○ B. 2
    ○ C. 33
    ○ D. 12

16. A rectangular table has a length of 10 feet and a width of 6 feet. What is the area of the table?

    ○ A. 61
    ○ B. 32
    ○ C. 60
    ○ D. 16

Division

Multiplying involves adding an equal number of groups multiple times. For division, you have to figure out how many groups the whole needs to be split into and the size of each group. When you divide, you split the whole into equal parts. There are two types of division.

Size of Each Group (Partitive Division)

If you know the whole amount and the number of groups in a problem, you can figure out the size of each group.

For example, if 3 children equally share 12 pencils, how many pencils does each child get?

To solve this problem you have to divide the 12 pencils into three equal groups to figure out how many pencils each child gets. In this problem, the whole is made up of 12 pencils. We also know the number of groups the whole needs to be split into. This is three groups. What we don't know is how many pencils make up the size of each group.

Example

There is $36. Six children equally share the money. How much money does each child get?

$$\$36 \div 6 = \$6$$

$6 $6 $6 $6 $6 $6

To solve this problem, you have to equally divide $36 among the 6 children. You can give each child a dollar until all the money is divided into six piles. You can also use your multiplication facts to figure out the answer: 6 × 6 = 36. You know that $36 can be equally divided into six equal groups.

Number of Groups the Whole Is Divided Into (Measurement Division)

If you know the whole amount and the size of each group the whole is divided into, you can figure out the number of groups.

Example

If there is a 12-inch piece of ribbon, how many 4-inch pieces can it be cut into?

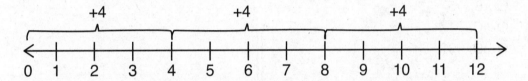

Division problems are related to multiplication. For example, if you know that 4 × 7 = 28, you can figure out that 28 ÷ 4 = 7. Seven groups of four make twenty-eight. This means that if 28 is divided into 4 equal groups, it will make 7 groups. This is called a **fact family** because they are related. You can multiply the numbers 4 and 7 to get 28. If you divide 28 by 4 you get 7. If you divide 28 by 7 you get 4.

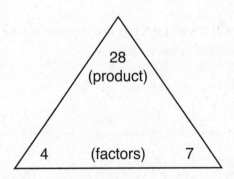

Division Practice Problems

(Answers can be found on pages 224–226.)

1. There are 25 apples. Five people share them equally. How many apples does each person get?

   O A. 4
   O B. 3
   O C. 30
   O D. 5

2. There are 16 cookies. Two children share them equally. How many cookies does each child get?

   O A. 8
   O B. 5
   O C. 17
   O D. 32

3. Zack has $20. He wants to buy movie tickets for his friends. Each ticket costs $4? How many tickets can Zack buy?

   O A. 3
   O B. 24
   O C. 5
   O D. 4

4. There are 28 pennies. If these pennies are divided into 7 equal groups, how many pennies will be in each group?

   O A. 5
   O B. 4
   O C. 3
   O D. 8

5. There are 30 hot dogs. Each child eats 2 hot dogs. How many children eat hot dogs?

○ A. 12
○ B. 21
○ C. 15
○ D. 8

6. Ms. Jane has 21 books. She gives each child 3 books. How many children get books?

○ A. 6
○ B. 24
○ C. 7
○ D. 5

7. Does replacing the unknown number with 6 make the equation true?

Select **YES** or **NO** for each equation.

	YES	NO
$6 \times \square = 36$		
$5 \times \square = 30$		
$64 \div \square = 8$		
$60 \div \square = 10$		

8. Which equation has the same unknown value as $18 \div 9 = \square$?

    ○ A. $6 \div 18 = \square$

    ○ B. $\square \times 4 = 12$

    ○ C. $12 \times \square = 24$

    ○ D. $\square \div 4 = 28$

9. Decide if each equation is true or false. Place a check mark to indicate **TRUE** or **FALSE** for each equation.

	TRUE	FALSE
$2 \times 5 = 5 \div 2$		
$3 \times 8 = 48 \div 2$		
$10 \times 3 = 25 \div 5$		

10. What unknown number makes this equation true?

$4 \times \square = 28$

    ○ A. 8

    ○ B. 7

    ○ C. 2

    ○ D. 6

Two-Step Word Problems

You have to use problem solving strategies to solve word problems. First, you have to figure out what the problem is asking you to do. Next, you have to decide which operation (+, −, ×, or ÷) to use to solve the problem.

> ### Here are some problem solving strategies:
>
> > Understand the problem. Figure out what information is given and what you have to do.
>
> > Draw a picture to visualize the problem.
>
> > Come up with a plan.
>
> > Solve the problem.

Using a Letter for the Unknown Quantity

In the previous examples, we used a box to represent the unknown quantity. You can also use a letter to represent the unknown quantity. This is called a variable.

For example, in $3 \times s = 12$, the letter s can represent the unknown quantity. s in this number sentence represents 4 since $3 \times 4 = 12$.

Two-Step Word Practice Problems

(Answers can be found on pages 226–227.)

1. Latisha has some marbles. Jose has 26 marbles. They have 45 marbles all together. How many marbles does Latisha have? Which of the following equations represents the problem? Note: The letter *m* is used to represent how many marbles Latisha has.

   ○ A. $m + 26 = 45$
   ○ B. $45 + 26 = m$
   ○ C. $m \div 26 = 45$
   ○ D. $m \times 26 = 45$

2. Jen had $45. She gave $25 to her brother and bought a T-shirt for $7. How much money does she have left? Show your work.

   ○ A. $49
   ○ B. $25
   ○ C. $13
   ○ D. $28

3. Mrs. Jones's third-grade class is having a bake sale. The prices of the items are listed below.

Bake Sale Prices

Cupcakes	$2
Soda	$1
Pie	$5

The class sold 10 cupcakes, 8 sodas, and 4 pies. How much money did they make? Show your work.

4. Sarah and John built a rectangular four-sided fence for their dog. The perimeter of the fence is 100 feet. One side of the fence measures 30 feet. A different side measures 30 feet. The third side measures 20 feet.

Part A. Draw and label a diagram of the fence. Use a letter to represent the unknown side length.

Part B. What is the length of the unknown side? Show your work or explain how you know.

5. Cameron had 120 Hot Wheels cars. He gave half of his cars to his sister and 2 to his friend. How many cars does Cameron have left?

Arithmetic Patterns

You should notice patterns in the multiplication table and the 100 chart and be able to explain these patterns using properties of operations. This means, you should be able to figure out a pattern and explain it by figuring out the rule in the pattern. You can describe it using addition, subtraction, multiplication, or division. For example, take a look at the 100 chart. What pattern do you notice?

1	2	3	4	5	6	7	8	9	10
11	12	13	14	15	16	17	18	19	20
21	22	23	24	25	26	27	28	29	30
31	32	33	34	35	36	37	38	39	40
41	42	43	44	45	46	47	48	49	50
51	52	53	54	55	56	57	58	59	60
61	62	63	64	65	66	67	68	69	70
71	72	73	74	75	76	77	78	79	80
81	82	83	84	85	86	87	88	89	90
91	92	93	94	95	96	97	98	99	100

You may notice that when you go down the 100 chart, the amount increases by 10. So, you are adding 10 every time you go down the 100 chart. Here is another example: If you start at 24 and add 4 each time, you will have a sequence of numbers, such as 24, 28, 32, 36, ... The rule is adding 4 to a number or +4.

You can also look for patterns in addition and multiplication tables. For example, all numbers multiplied by 2 are even numbers.

+	0	1	2	3	4	5	6	7	8	9	10
0	0	1	2	3	4	5	6	7	8	9	10
1	1	2	3	4	5	6	7	8	9	10	11
2	2	3	4	5	6	7	8	9	10	11	12
3	3	4	5	6	7	8	9	10	11	12	13
4	4	5	6	7	8	9	10	11	12	13	14
5	5	6	7	8	9	10	11	12	13	14	15
6	6	7	8	9	10	11	12	13	14	15	16
7	7	8	9	10	11	12	13	14	15	16	17
8	8	9	10	11	12	13	14	15	16	17	18
9	9	10	11	12	13	14	15	16	17	18	19
10	10	11	12	13	14	15	16	17	18	19	20

×	1	2	3	4	5	6	7	8	9	10	11	12
1	1	2	3	4	5	6	7	8	9	10	11	12
2	2	4	6	8	10	12	14	16	18	20	22	24
3	3	6	9	12	15	18	21	24	27	30	33	36
4	4	8	12	16	20	24	28	32	36	40	44	48
5	5	10	15	20	25	30	35	40	45	50	55	60
6	6	12	18	24	30	36	42	48	54	60	66	72
7	7	14	21	28	35	42	49	56	63	70	77	84
8	8	16	24	32	40	48	56	64	72	80	88	96
9	9	18	27	36	45	54	63	72	81	90	99	108
10	10	20	30	40	50	60	70	80	90	100	110	120
11	11	22	33	44	55	66	77	88	99	110	121	132
12	12	24	36	48	60	72	84	96	108	120	132	144

Patterns can also be represented in a table. You can figure out the patterns for what is the In number and the Out number by figuring out the rule. For example, the table below represents the rule of adding 3 to a number.

Rule
+3

In	Out
5	8
6	9
7	10
8	11

5 + 3 = 8

6 + 3 = 9

7 + 3 = 10

8 + 3 = 11

Arithmetic Pattern Practice Problems

(Answers can be found on pages 227–228.)

1. Select the missing number in the pattern.

   1, 11, 21, 31, 41, ____

   ○ A. 61
   ○ B. 51
   ○ C. 31
   ○ D. 12

2. Select the missing number in the pattern.

   3, 6, ____, 12, 15

   ○ A. 4
   ○ B. 5
   ○ C. 7
   ○ D. 9

3. Select the missing number in the pattern.

   44, 42, 40, 38, ____

   ○ A. 43
   ○ B. 41
   ○ C. 36
   ○ D. 34

4. Which set of numbers shows the rule below?

   Add 2

   ○ A. 3, 6, 9, 12
   ○ B. 3, 5, 7, 9
   ○ C. 2, 4, 5, 8
   ○ D. 4, 8, 16, 20

5. What is the rule for the pattern in the In and Out table?

Rule
?

In	Out
3	7
4	8
5	9
6	10

- O A. +2
- O B. +3
- O C. +4
- O D. −2

6. Fill in the chart with the missing number using the rule below.

Rule
× 2

In	Out
2	4
4	8
6	?
8	16

- O A. 12
- O B. 4
- O C. 9
- O D. 6

Operations and Algebraic Thinking Chapter Review

(Answers can be found on pages 228–231.)

1. Christopher wants to buy 3 packs of Pokémon cards. Each pack costs $7. How much money does Christopher need to buy 3 packs of Pokémon cards?

   ○ A. $21
   ○ B. $11
   ○ C. $30
   ○ D. $36

2. There are 4 children. Each child eats 2 lollipops. How many lollipops do all four children eat? Which of the following expressions represents this problem?

   ○ A. 5×1
   ○ B. 4×2
   ○ C. 2×5
   ○ D. 6×2

3. $9 \times 3 = ?$

   ○ A. 27
   ○ B. 25
   ○ C. 13
   ○ D. 12

4. Which expression is equal to 5×8?

   ○ A. $(2 \times 7) + (2 \times 7)$
   ○ B. $(4 \times 7) + (4 \times 7)$
   ○ C. $(7 \times 4) + (7 \times 4)$
   ○ D. $(5 \times 3) + (5 \times 5)$

5. The addition sentence $6 + 6 + 6$ has the same value as which of the following expressions?

   ○ A. $24 \div 8$
   ○ B. 3×6
   ○ C. $6 + 3$
   ○ D. $8 + 3$

6. Which array represents 4 × 3?

O A.

O B.

O C.

O D.

7. There are 24 strawberries. Eight people share the strawberries equally. How many strawberries does each person get?

O A. 4

O B. 3

O C. 30

O D. 5

8. There are 16 ounces of sugar. Each batch of cookies uses 4 ounces of sugar.
   How many batches of cookies can be made from 16 ounces of sugar?

   O A. 6
   O B. 4
   O C. 7
   O D. 5

9. Does replacing the unknown number with 4 make the equation true?
   Select **YES** or **NO** for each equation.

	YES	NO
$6 \times \square = 24$		
$5 \times \square = 30$		
$14 \div \square = 8$		
$60 \div \square = 10$		

10. Decide if each equation is true or false. Put a check mark to indicate
    TRUE or **FALSE** for each equation.

	TRUE	FALSE
$3 \times 5 = 15 + 0$		
$4 \times 2 = 16 \div 2$		
$10 \times 4 = 25 \div 5$		

11. Bob has some gumballs. Juan has 6 gumballs. Together they have 21 gumballs. How many gumballs does Bob have? Which of the following equations represents the problem? Note: The letter m is used to represent how many gumballs Bob has.

    ○ A. $m + 6 = 21$

    ○ B. $6 + 21 = m$

    ○ C. $m \div 26 = 6$

    ○ D. $m \times 26 = 45$

12. Write the missing number in the pattern.

5, 10, 15, 20, 25, ____

    ○ A. 26

    ○ B. 45

    ○ C. 31

    ○ D. 30

13. Write the missing number in the pattern.

7, 14, 21, ____, 35

    ○ A. 28

    ○ B. 29

    ○ C. 30

    ○ D. 31

14. Which set of numbers shows the rule below?

Add 3

    ○ A. 3, 6, 9, 12

    ○ B. 2, 5, 5, 9

    ○ C. 3, 4, 4, 5, 8

    ○ D. 4, 8, 12, 21

15. What is the rule for the pattern in the In and Out table?

Rule
?

In	Out
4	8
5	9
6	10
7	11

○ A. +2
○ B. +3
○ C. +4
○ D. −2

Progress Checklist

Algebraic Thinking	Needs work	Working On	Mastered
Multiplication Equal groups and number of groups Meaning of the multiplication symbols Equal sets Arrays Number lines			
Multiplication Properties Commutative Associative Distributive			

Progress Checklist (continued)

Algebraic Thinking	Needs work	Working On	Mastered
Division Size of group times number of groups			
Partitive Division (size of groups)			
Measurement Division Find the number of groups if the whole and the size are given.			
Patterns in the Multiplication Table			
Multiplication Facts 1 2 3 4 5 6 7 8 9 10 11 12			
Using a Letter to Represent an Unknown Quantity			
Multiplication and Division Fact Family			
Two-Step Word Problems			
Patterns			

Number and Operations in Base Ten

Whole Number Place Value

Place Value

Each digit in a number represents a value depending on its place in the number. For example, consider the number 123. The digit 1 represents the 100s place. The digit 2 represents the 10s place, which is made up of two sets of ten units. The digit 3 represents the 1s place, and is three single units.

The table below represents the value of each digit in the number 123.

100s Place	10s Place	1s Place
	Rod = 10 Rod = 10	

The number 123 is made up of the following:

One 100s unit (100)

Two 10s units (10 + 10. These numbers add up to the number 20.)

Three 1s units (1 + 1 + 1. These numbers add up to the number 3.)

123 = 100 + 20 + 3

Note: The value of the digits increases by multiples of 10 as you move to the left from the decimal point. For example, 100 represents 10 times as many units as 10 units.

Whole Number Place Value Practice Problems

(Answers can be found on page 231.)

1. What is the value of the digit 8 in the number 78?

   O A.   8 one units
   O B.   8 ten units
   O C.   80
   O D.   8 hundred units

2. What is the value of the digit 7 in the number 375?

   O A.   7 one units
   O B.   7 ten units
   O C.   7 thousand units
   O D.   7 hundred units

3. What number does the following diagram represent?

100s Place	10s Place	1s Place
	Rod = 10	

   O A.   12
   O B.   22
   O C.   2
   O D.   112

4. What number does the following diagram represent?

100s Place	10s Place	1s Place
	Rod = 10 Rod = 10	
	Rod = 10 Rod = 10	

- O A. 421
- O B. 241
- O C. 142
- O D. 42

5. Which of the following expressions represents the number 125?

- O A. 100 + 200 + 5
- O B. 200 + 100 + 5
- O C. 100 + 20 + 5
- O D. 100 + 20 + 50

Rounding to the Nearest 10 or 100

Rounding is a great tool to use when estimating and adding numbers. For example, you can estimate the value of 19 + 9 by rounding 19 up to 20 and rounding 9 up to 10. It is easier to add 20 + 10 and figure out that the estimated answer should be about 30.

Rounding to the Nearest 10 or 0

- Round numbers 5 or greater to 10
- Round numbers 4 or lower to 0

For example, the number 6 can be rounded up to 10. The number 3 can be rounded down to 0.

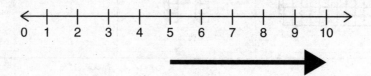

Rounding to the Nearest 10 or 0 Practice Problems

(Answers can be found on page 231.)

Round up to 10 or down to 0?

1. 9

    O   A.   Round up to 10
    O   B.   Round down to 0

2. 4

    O   A.   Round up to 10
    O   B.   Round down to 0

3. 7

    O   A.   Round up to 10
    O   B.   Round down to 0

4. 2

   ○ A.   Round up to 10

   ○ B.   Round down to 0

5. 6

   ○ A.   Round up to 10

   ○ B.   Round down to 0

Rounding to the Nearest 10

Round up to the nearest 10 when digits in the ones place is equal to or greater than 5

1	2	3	4	5	6	7	8	9	10
11	12	13	14	15	16	17	18	19	20
21	22	23	24	25	26	27	28	29	30
31	32	33	34	35	36	37	38	39	40
41	42	43	44	45	46	47	48	49	50
51	52	53	54	55	56	57	58	59	60
61	62	63	64	65	66	67	68	69	70
71	72	73	74	75	76	77	78	79	80
81	82	83	84	85	86	87	88	89	90
91	92	93	94	95	96	97	98	99	100

A two-digit number that has a digit in the ones place can be rounded up or down to the nearest digit.

Any number in the ones place that is greater than 5 can be rounded up to the nearest 10. For example, the number 38 can be rounded up to 40. The number 47 can be rounded up to 50.

When the number in the ones place is less than 5, then round down to the nearest 10.

For example, the number 94 can be rounded down to 90. The number 73 can be rounded down to 70, and the number 22 can be rounded down to 20.

Rounding to the Nearest 10 Practice Problems

(Answers can be found on pages 231–232.)

Round up or down to the nearest 10.

1. 35

- O A. 36
- O B. 40
- O C. 30
- O D. 34

2. 76

- O A. 80
- O B. 100
- O C. 70
- O D. 60

3. 28

- O A. 30
- O B. 80
- O C. 20
- O D. 82

4. 84

- O A. 85
- O B. 90
- O C. 80
- O D. 48

5. 32

- O A. 33
- O B. 40
- O C. 30
- O D. 35

Rounding to the Nearest 100

When rounding to the nearest 100, look at the number in the tens place and decide if it is 50 or greater. If it is equal to or greater than 50, round up to the nearest 100.

If the number is 49 or less, round down to the nearest 100.

For example, 253 can be rounded up to 300 since 53 is greater than 50. 123 can be rounded down to 100 since 23 is less than 50.

Examples

100s Place	10s Place	1s Place
2	5	7

The number 257 can be thought of as 200 + 50 + 7 or 200 + 57. 57 is greater than 50, so round up to the nearest 100. This would make it 300 in the 100s place.

100s Place	10s Place	1s Place
3	0	0

Refer to the following table when rounding up or down to the nearest 100.

Round down	To	Round up	To
100–149	100	150–199	200
200–249	200	250–299	300
300–349	300	350–399	400
400–449	400	450–499	500
500–549	500	550–599	600
600–649	600	650–699	700
700–749	700	750–799	800
800–849	800	850–899	900
900–949	900	950–999	1,000

Rounding to the Nearest 100 Practice Problems

(Answers can be found on page 232.)

Round up or down to the nearest 100.

1. 259

- O A. 300
- O B. 400
- O C. 200
- O D 250

2. 762

- O A. 267
- O B. 760
- O C. 800
- O D. 700

3. 923

- O A. 900
- O B. 1,000
- O C 920
- O D. 930

4. 555

- O A. 600
- O B. 500
- O C. 660
- O D. 549

5. 942

- O A. 940
- O B. 902
- O C. 900
- O D. 100

Big Ideas of Addition

You can solve addition problems using many different strategies. Knowing the properties of how numbers work can help you find easier ways to solve problems. Find a method that works best for you. When you understand how numbers work, then it is easier to break numbers apart and put them together to add and subtract. This will help you solve problems, rather than simply memorizing formulas.

Properties of Addition

Commutative

If you change the order of the numbers that you are adding or if you move the numbers around, the total amount will still be the same. For example, if you are trying to add $3 + 7$, the order in which you add the numbers does not matter. The answer is the same whether you added 7 to 3 or 3 to 7.

$$3 + 7 = 10$$

$$7 + 3 = 10$$

Associative

You can group numbers together and add them in any order and the sum will be the same. For example, if you are adding $25 + 26 + 25$, you can add $25 + 25$ and get 50, and then add 26 more to get 76. You can also add 25 and 26 together to get 51, and then add 25 more to get 76. In other words, you can add any set of numbers in any order and combine them to get the same sum.

$$25 + 26 + 25 = 76$$

$$(25 + 26) + 25 = 76$$

$$(25 + 25) + 26 = 76$$

Identity

You can add a zero to any number, and the number will stay the same. For example, if you add $0 + 7$, the answer will be 7.

Relationship Between Addition and Subtraction

Addition

Solve Addition Problems by Using Place Value and Properties of Operations

You can break numbers apart to make easier numbers to combine. When first starting to learn addition, it may help to use place value blocks to help you visualize the numbers.

Example

$$52 + 53$$

One way is to break the number down into friendlier numbers so that they are easier to combine. Add the groups of ten together and combine the groups of one together.

$$50 + 50 + 2 + 3 = 100 + 5$$

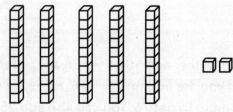

Rod = 10 Rod = 10 Rod = 10 Rod = 10 Rod = 10

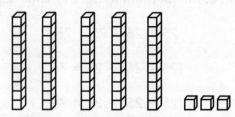

Rod = 10 Rod = 10 Rod = 10 Rod = 10 Rod = 10

$$52 + 53 = 105$$

Addition Problems with Re-grouping

If adding 27 + 19, combine the tens together and then combine the ones together. Substitute 10 ones for one 10-Rod, and then add the remainder.

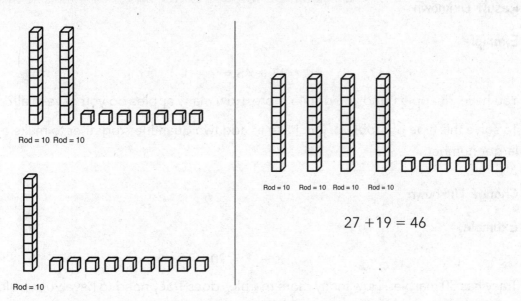

Rod = 10   Rod = 10

Rod = 10

Rod = 10   Rod = 10   Rod = 10   Rod = 10

$27 + 19 = 46$

Standard Algorithm

Example

$$
\begin{array}{r}
52 \\
+53 \\
\hline
105
\end{array}
$$

Types of Addition Problems

There are different types of addition problems.

Result Unknown

Example

$$25 + 45 = ?$$

You have 25 apples, and you get 45 more. How many apples do you have in all?

To solve this type of problem, you have to add two quantities together to make a larger number.

Change Unknown

Example

$$30 + ? = 90$$

Tracy has 30 marbles. How many more marbles does Tracy need to have 90 marbles?

To solve this problem, you have to figure out the missing amount. You can use several strategies to solve this problem. One strategy you can use is to think of it as a bar diagram. Think about what part is missing.

30	?

90

You can also think about this question as a subtraction problem.

$$90 - 30 = ?$$

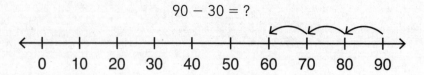

Start Unknown

Example

$$? + \$78 = \$150$$

Tom had some money. His dad gave him $78 more. Tom now has $150. How much money did Tom have before his dad gave him $78?

To solve this problem, you have to figure out how much money Tom had to start. To do this, you can set it up as a subtraction problem: $150 − $78 = ?

Addition Practice Problems

(Answers can be found on pages 232–233.)

Add the following numbers.

1. 20 + 30 = ?

    O A.   60

    O B.   50

    O C.   23

    O D.   230

2. 50 + 14 = ?

    O A.   64

    O B.   54

    O C.   514

    O D.   10

3. 62 + 27 = ?

    O A.   92

    O B.   98

    O C.   64

    O D.   89

4. 74 + 23 + 15 = ?

    O A.   95

    O B.   112

    O C.   107

    O D.   109

5. 14 + 9 + 74 = ?

    O A.   88

    O B.   95

    O C.   97

    O D.   149

6. Sam had 20 blocks and he was given some more. He now has 37 blocks. How many more blocks did he get?

   O A. 57
   O B. 17
   O C. 50
   O D. 39

7. Pam had some money. Her mom gave her $15 more. She now has $27. How much money did Pam start with?

   O A. $42
   O B. $37
   O C. $43
   O D. $12

8. Tyrone had 26 crayons. He was given 25 more. How many crayons does Tyrone have now?

   O A. 51
   O B. 47
   O C. 46
   O D. 65

9. Sharon had some pencils. Her teacher gave her 22 more. She now has 46 pencils. How many pencils did Sharon start with?

   O A. 68
   O B. 26
   O C. 24
   O D. 48

10. Sameer has $22, and his brother gives him $27 more? How much money does Sameer have now?

   O A. $37
   O B. $49
   O C. $29
   O D. $47

Types of Subtraction Problems

Result Unknown

Example

$$25 - 14 = ?$$

Shera has 25 peanuts. She gives 14 peanuts to her sister. How many peanuts does Shera have left?

Change Unknown

Example

$$48 - ? = 26$$

There are 48 meatballs. The dog eats some of the meatballs, and now there are only 26 left. How many meatballs did the dog eat?

Start Unknown

Example

$$? - 13 = 27$$

A boy has some balloons. He gives 13 balloons away. He now has 27 left. How many balloons did he start with?

Subtraction Practice Problems

(Answers can be found on page 233.)

1. There are 45 bananas. 15 bananas are eaten. How many bananas are left?

   O A. 65
   O B. 30
   O C. 55
   O D. 46

2. The bakery had 31 pies. They sold some of the pies and now have 15 left. How many pies did the bakery sell?

   O A. 46
   O B. 26
   O C. 16
   O D. 21

3. Savanah had some money. She gave $12 away. She now has $15 left. How much money did Savanah start with?

   O A. $21
   O B. $27
   O C. $35
   O D. $72

Multiplying by Multiples of 10

When you multiply a number by 10, you are multiplying the number by groups of 10.

For example, the number 3 × 10 is made up of 3 groups of 10, which equals 30.

3 Groups of 10

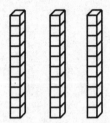

3 groups of 10 is the same as 10 + 10 + 10 = 30

If you multiply 2 × 20, think about what the number 20 means. If you use base 10 blocks, you see that 20 is made up of 2 base 10 blocks. So, you will need 2 sets of base 10 blocks.

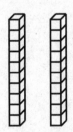

Notice when you multiply any number by 10, you add zero to the end of it because it represents the number of groups of 10.

Groups of 10 Practice Problems

(Answers can be found on page 234.)

Find the product.

1. 2 × 30 = ?

    O A. 60

    O B. 600

    O C. 50

    O D. 500

2. 5 × 20 = ?

    O A. 10

    O B. 70

    O C. 100

    O D. 700

3. 7 × 20 = ?

    O A. 140

    O B. 14

    O C. 90

    O D. 900

4. 3 × 10 = ?

    O A. 300

    O B. 40

    O C. 30

    O D. 400

5. 4 × 20 = ?

    O A. 60

    O B. 800

    O C. 80

    O D. 600

Number and Operations in Base 10 Chapter Review

(Answers can be found on pages 234–235.)

1. What is the value of the digit 6 in the number 96?

   O   A.   6 one units
   O   B.   6 ten units
   O   C.   60
   O   D.   6 hundred units

2. What is the value of the digit 5 in the number 526?

   O   A.   5 one units
   O   B.   5 ten units
   O   C.   50
   O   D.   5 hundred units

3. What number does the following diagram represent?

100s Place	10s Place	1s Place
	Rod = 10 Rod = 10 Rod = 10	

   O   A.   32
   O   B.   22
   O   C.   12
   O   D.   320

4. Which of the following expressions represents the number 89?

   O   A.   80 + 9
   O   B.   50 + 80
   O   C.   100 + 20 + 5
   O   D.   89 + 20

5. Round 7 up or down?

    O A.   Round up to 10

    O B.   Round down to 0

6. Round 325 to the nearest 100.

    O A.   300

    O B.   260

    O C.   200

    O D.   250

7. $45 + 26 = ?$

    O A.   60

    O B.   66

    O C.   23

    O D.   71

8. $10 + 16 + 28 = ?$

    O A.   54

    O B.   44

    O C.   26

    O D.   75

9. Mary had 15 paperclips. She was given some more paperclips. She now has 27 paperclips. How many more paperclips did Mary get?

    O A.   15

    O B.   17

    O C.   12

    O D.   26

10. $4 \times 10 = ?$

    ○ A. 40

    ○ B. 400

    ○ C. 44

    ○ D. 120

11. There are 32 oranges. 5 oranges are eaten. How many oranges are left?

    ○ A. 37

    ○ B. 27

    ○ C. 55

    ○ D. 46

12. The pet store had 42 hamsters. They sold some of the hamsters, and now they have 12 left. How many hamsters did the pet store sell?

    ○ A. 46

    ○ B. 26

    ○ C. 30

    ○ D. 21

13. Scott had some bags of chips. He gave 7 bags away. He now has 19 bags left. How many bags of chips did Scott start with?

    ○ A. 26

    ○ B. 27

    ○ C. 19

    ○ D. 72

14. Craig had some rubber bands. He got 9 more rubber bands, and now he has 67 rubber bands. How many rubber bands did Craig start out with?

    ○ A. 89

    ○ B. 58

    ○ C. 69

    ○ D. 45

15. Yin had $17. She got $58 more. How much money does Yin have now?

- ○ A. $62
- ○ B. $89
- ○ C. $75
- ○ D. $59

Progress Checklist

	Needs work	Working on	Mastered
Place Value			
1s place			
10s place			
100s place			
Rounding			
10s place			
100s place			
Addition Within 100			
Algorithm			
Addition Problem Types			
Result Unknown			
Change Unknown			
Start Unknown			
Subtraction Problem Types			
Result Unknown			
Change Unknown			
Start Unknown			
Multiply by Multiples of 10			

Number and Operations— Fractions

CHAPTER 11

FRACTION VOCABULARY

> **Fraction**—a number that refers to part of a whole.
For example, the fraction $\frac{1}{2}$ represents 1 out of 2 parts. If a pizza is cut into 2 equal size pieces, 1 of these pieces represents $\frac{1}{2}$ of the pizza.

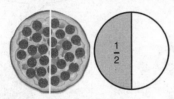

> **Numerator**—the top number of the fraction. It represents the number of parts of the whole. For example, in the fraction $\frac{1}{2}$, 1 represents the numerator. It is one part of the 2 equal pieces.

> **Denominator**—the bottom number of the fraction. It represents the total number of equal parts the whole is divided into. For example, in the fraction $\frac{1}{2}$, 2 represents how many pieces the whole is divided into.

Example:

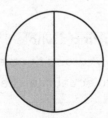

$\frac{1}{4}$ ← Numerator
← Denominator

The whole is divided into 4 equal parts. One of the parts is shaded and represents the fraction $\frac{1}{4}$. The 1 refers to the numerator. The 4 represents the denominator and is the number of equal parts the whole is divided into.

Big Ideas for Understanding Fractions

You will be using these big ideas when learning fractions.

Unit

A unit represents the whole in a problem. When working with fractions, it is important to look at the whole in order to solve problems. The whole can take many forms. For example, it can be made up of one pizza, two pizzas, a bag of chips, 12 individual eggs, a carton of eggs, or even half a dozen eggs. Understanding what makes up the whole is helpful for seeing the parts of the whole.

Partition

This is the process of **cutting** or **sorting** a whole unit into equal parts. Whole units, such as a pizza, are cut into pieces. A group of objects that make up a whole, such as a dozen eggs, can be sorted into equal piles. Each pile is made up of equal sets of objects.

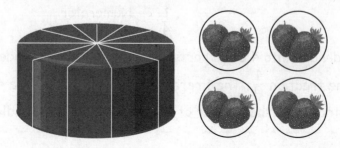

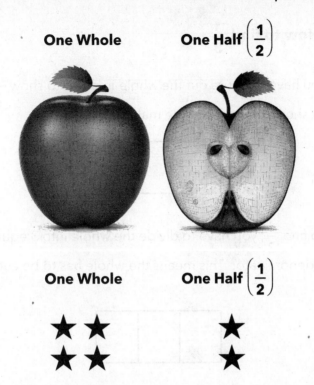

One Whole   **One Half** $\left(\dfrac{1}{2}\right)$

One Whole   **One Half** $\left(\dfrac{1}{2}\right)$

Note: The pictures above show a whole and a half. One whole unit, an apple, is cut into two equal parts. The other whole unit made up of 4 stars is sorted into two equal groups (sets) of 2 stars. They both show the fraction $\dfrac{1}{2}$ of the original whole unit. The top number, 1, in the fraction shows that there is one whole. This is the numerator. It refers to one part of the whole that has been divided into 2 equal parts. The bottom number, 2, represents the denominator, or how many parts the whole is divided into. In the fraction $\dfrac{1}{2}$, the whole unit has been divided into 2 equal parts.

Example (Area Model)

This is a third.

$$\dfrac{1}{3}$$

Step-by-Step—How to find $\frac{1}{3}$

STEP 1 First, you have to figure out the whole in order to show $\frac{1}{3}$ of the whole. The picture below shows that a rectangle makes up the whole.

STEP 2 Next, to find $\frac{1}{3}$, you have to divide the whole into 3 equal parts. The 3 in the fraction is the denominator. This means the whole has to be cut into 3 equal parts.

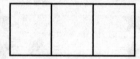

STEP 3 Lastly, you have to show the top number (numerator) in order to figure out how many parts to color. In this case, you only have to color one piece because the top number is 1. It shows 1 out of the 3 parts of the whole.

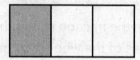

Note: The non-colored part shows $\frac{2}{3}$ of the whole.

Example (Set Model)

Find $\frac{1}{3}$ of the set of 6 marbles.

Step-by-Step

STEP 1   It is important to know that the whole is made up of 6 marbles.

STEP 2   In order to find $\frac{1}{3}$, you have to first look at the bottom number of the fraction. This number will tell you how many equal parts the whole must be divided into.

STEP 3   The bottom number (denominator) is 3. This means the whole must be sorted into 3 equal groups.

STEP 4   The next step is to figure out the top number. The top number of $\frac{1}{3}$ is 1. It is equal to one of the three groups.

$\frac{1}{3}$ represents 1 out of the three groups the whole is divided into. It represents $\frac{1}{3}$ of the whole.

Equivalency (Equal Size Pieces)

The pieces are equal if they have the same area.

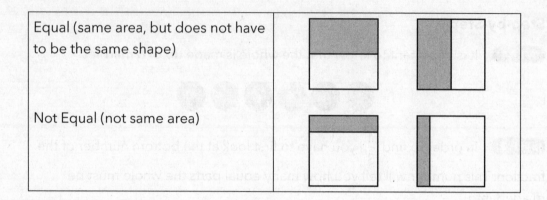

| Equal (same area, but does not have to be the same shape) | |
| Not Equal (not same area) | |

Pieces versus Fractions

When a whole unit is divided into equal parts, the parts can be counted as whole numbers. For example, a rectangle is cut into 2 equal parts. The rectangle is made up of two equal pieces. One of these pieces shows $\frac{1}{2}$ of the whole rectangle.

When you think about how the piece is part of the whole, then you are thinking about the piece as a fraction.

Types of Models to Represent Fractions

Drawing models of fractions can be helpful to solve problems. Listed below are the types of models that can be used to show real-world fractions.

Area Model

A whole unit that can be cut into parts (e.g., a pizza or pie).

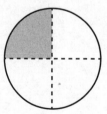

Set Model

The whole unit is made up of many objects, such as a set of balls. If there are six balls in the set, then half of the set is made up of 3 balls. You have to sort the balls into equal groups to figure out the fraction.

Number Line

Number lines can be used to show the length of units such as a piece of wood, a sandwich, or a piece of ribbon. To divide the whole unit into equal parts, you have to divide it into equal size segments.

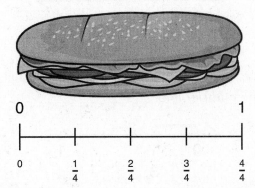

The whole unit is the distance from 0 to 1 on the number line. Each fraction represents a segment on the number line. For example, if you want to figure out where $\frac{1}{4}$ lies on the number line, you have to divide the whole unit into 4 equal segments. The bottom number of the fraction (denominator) is 4. The top number of the fraction (numerator) is 1. Each segment represents $\frac{1}{4}$ of the whole unit. In the example above, the whole number is divided into fourths. Each additional segment adds $\frac{1}{4}$ of the length. So, you can count $\frac{1}{4}$, $\frac{2}{4}$, $\frac{3}{4}$, and $\frac{4}{4}$. This means $\frac{2}{4}$ is made up of two $\frac{1}{4}$ segments, $\frac{3}{4}$ is made up of three $\frac{1}{4}$ segments, and $\frac{4}{4}$ is made up of four $\frac{1}{4}$ segments and is equal to one whole.

Example (Linear Model)

Show $\frac{1}{3}$ on a number line.

Step-by-Step

STEP 1 First create a number line with one unit.

STEP 2 The bottom number in the fraction tells you how many equal parts you have to divide the whole into. The bottom number (denominator) in $\frac{1}{3}$ is 3. This means that you have to divide the whole unit into 3 equal segments.

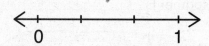

STEP 3 Look at the top number (the numerator). It is 1. This means it represents 1 of the 3 segments on the number line.

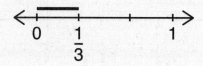

Review Questions
- What is a fraction?
- What do the numerator and denominator represent?
- What kinds of units are there?
- Why is it important to identify the unit?
- What is partitioning?

Identifying Fractions Practice Problems

(Answers can be found on pages 235–236.)

Solve the following problems.

1. Which **two** models represent the fraction $\frac{1}{2}$?

   ☐ A.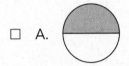

   ☐ B.

   ☐ C.

   ☐ D.

2. There are 4 pies. One is a blueberry pie, and the rest are apple pies. What fraction of the total pies do the apple pies represent?

   ○ A. $\frac{1}{4}$

   ○ B. $\frac{2}{4}$

   ○ C. $\frac{3}{4}$

   ○ D. $\frac{1}{3}$

3. Emily cut an orange into six equal pieces. She ate $\frac{1}{6}$ of the orange. How many pieces are left?

   ○ A. 5
   ○ B. 6
   ○ C. 1
   ○ D. 0

4. Which **two** models represent $\frac{1}{3}$?

□ A.

□ B.

□ C.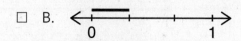

□ D.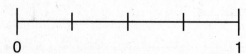

5. Show $\frac{3}{4}$ on the number line.

```
|-----+-----+-----+-----|
0                       1
```

6. Melissa has 1 whole pizza. She cuts it into 8 equal slices. She eats $\frac{1}{8}$ of the pizza. How many slices does Melissa have left?

O A. 8 slices
O B. 1 slice
O C. 7 slices
O D. 9 slices

7. Paul bought 2 tacos. He ate one and took the other one home. What fraction of the total tacos did Paul take home?

O A. $\frac{1}{4}$

O B. $\frac{1}{2}$

O C. $\frac{1}{3}$

O D. $\frac{1}{6}$

8. Juanita cut a cake into 4 equal parts. What fraction does two parts of the whole cake represent?

○ A. $\dfrac{4}{4}$

○ B. $\dfrac{1}{4}$

○ C. $\dfrac{2}{4}$

○ D. $\dfrac{3}{4}$

9. James cut a rope into 6 equal pieces. He gave 3 of the pieces to his friend. What fraction of the whole did he give to his friend?

○ A. $\dfrac{1}{3}$

○ B. $\dfrac{2}{6}$

○ C. $\dfrac{3}{6}$

○ D. $\dfrac{1}{4}$

10. The rectangle below has been cut into different sized parts. Label each part to indicate the size of the part relative to the whole. ($\dfrac{1}{2}, \dfrac{1}{4}, \dfrac{1}{8}$)

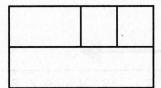

Expressing Whole Numbers as Fractions

Whole numbers can also be represented as fractions. The numerator tells you how many whole units there are. For example, the whole number 2 can be written as the fraction $\frac{2}{1}$. The top number (numerator) is made up of two whole units. The bottom number (denominator) is not divided into parts. It remains a whole.

Let's look at an example.

Example

You bought two oranges at the store. You can write this as $\frac{2}{1}$. The top number (numerator) represents that there are two oranges. The bottom number represents one whole orange. So the fraction $\frac{2}{1}$ means that there are two whole oranges.

$$\frac{2}{1}$$

You probably learned about number lines and know that numbers increase as you move to the right. Each number represents a whole unit.

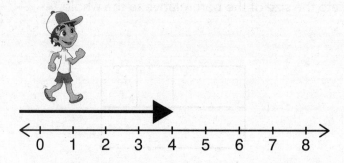

The numbers on the number line can be written as fractions. Each number on the number line tells you how many units there are. For example, look at the number 4 on the number line. It can be written as $\frac{4}{1}$. This means that there are four whole units.

Look at the pattern on the ruler below and notice the connection between whole numbers and fractions. You can write the whole numbers as fractions. The denominator will always be 1 because it means that the whole number remains as a whole unit without being divided.

$$\frac{1}{1} \quad \frac{2}{1} \quad \frac{3}{1} \quad \frac{4}{1} \quad \frac{5}{1} \quad \frac{6}{1} \quad \frac{7}{1}$$

A whole number can also be represented as a fraction when the top number (numerator) can be divided evenly by the bottom number (denominator).

Take for example, the fraction $\frac{2}{2}$. If you divide 2 by 2, you will get 1. In the fraction $\frac{4}{2}$, if you divide 4 by 2, you will get 2.

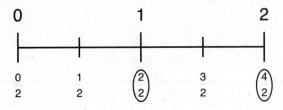

Mixed Numbers

You can also use mixed numbers to represent numbers on the number line. Notice on the ruler below, $\frac{3}{2}$ is the same as adding $\frac{1}{2}$ to the whole number 1.

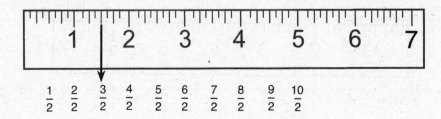

You can think about the fractions as you read across the number line as one half, two halves, three halves, four halves, five halves, and so on. Each fraction represents a single number.

Expressing Whole Numbers as Fractions Practice Problems

(Answers can be found on pages 236–237.)

1. Which **two** models represent $\frac{4}{3}$?

□ A.

□ B.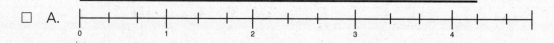

□ C.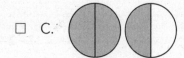

□ D.

2. Label the following number line with the fractions below:

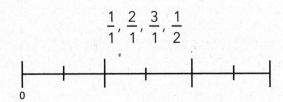

3. Choose **two** different ways to represent the shaded part of the circles.

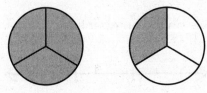

☐ A. $1\frac{1}{3}$

☐ B. $\frac{4}{6}$

☐ C. $\frac{2}{6}$

☐ D. $1\frac{2}{3}$

4. Represent the number 5 as a fraction.

○ A. $\frac{1}{5}$

○ B. $\frac{5}{1}$

○ C. $\frac{5}{0}$

○ D. 5 cannot be represented as a fraction.

5. Represent the number 6 as a fraction.

     ○ A. $\dfrac{1}{6}$

     ○ B. $\dfrac{6}{1}$

     ○ C. $\dfrac{6}{0}$

     ○ D. 6 cannot be represented as a fraction.

6. Represent the fraction $\dfrac{2}{1}$ on the number line.

7. Which **two** of the following fractions represent the number 2?

     ☐ A. $\dfrac{2}{1}$

     ☐ B. $\dfrac{4}{2}$

     ☐ C. $\dfrac{1}{2}$

     ☐ D. $\dfrac{2}{0}$

8. Which **two** of the following fractions represent the number 4?

     ☐ A. $\dfrac{4}{0}$

     ☐ B. $\dfrac{4}{1}$

     ☐ C. $\dfrac{1}{4}$

     ☐ D. $\dfrac{8}{2}$

Equivalent Fractions

Two fractions are equal or equivalent if they have the same area or length. On the number line, you will find that if the fractions are equal, they have the same length.

For example, $\dfrac{1}{2} = \dfrac{2}{4}$.

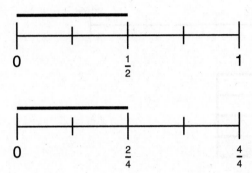

The area model below shows two equal fractions that have the same area. The important thing to notice is that the same unit is used in both situations.

Equivalent Fractions Practice Problems

(Answers can be found on pages 237–239.)

1. Which **three** models represent $\frac{1}{4}$?

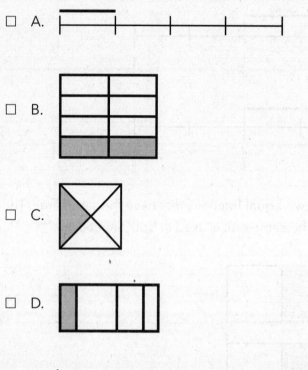

☐ A.

☐ B.

☐ C.

☐ D.

2. Shade $\frac{1}{2}$ of the model.

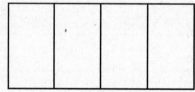

3. Shade $\frac{2}{3}$ of the model.

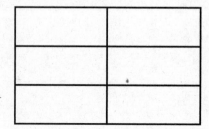

4. Which **two** of the following fractions are equivalent to $\frac{1}{2}$?

☐ A. $\frac{2}{1}$

☐ B. $\frac{2}{3}$

☐ C. $\frac{2}{4}$

☐ D. $\frac{3}{6}$

5. Jose got $\frac{2}{4}$ of a pizza, and Melissa got $\frac{4}{8}$ of a pizza. They have the same amount of pizza.

O A. True
O B. False

6. Tyrone got $\frac{4}{6}$ of a pie, and Tracy got $\frac{1}{3}$ of a pie. They have the same amount of pie.

O A. True
O B. False

7. Using the model below, show how $\frac{1}{3}$ and $\frac{2}{6}$ are equivalent.

$\frac{1}{3}$

$\frac{2}{6}$

8. Using the model below, show how $\frac{2}{4}$ and $\frac{4}{8}$ are equivalent.

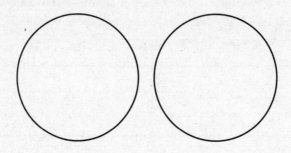

9. What number should be inserted to make the fractions equivalent?

$$\frac{1}{3} = \frac{?}{9}$$

- ○ A. 1
- ○ B. 2
- ○ C. 3
- ○ D. 4

10. What number should be inserted to make the fractions equivalent?

$$\frac{2}{6} = \frac{1}{?}$$

- ○ A. 1
- ○ B. 2
- ○ C. 3
- ○ D. 4

Comparing Fractions (>, <, =)

Comparing Fractions with the Same Denominators

When fractions have the same denominators, the top number (numerator) can be compared to determine the size of the fractions.

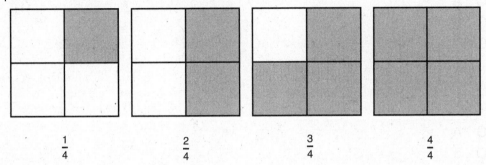

$$\frac{1}{4} \qquad\qquad \frac{2}{4} \qquad\qquad \frac{3}{4} \qquad\qquad \frac{4}{4}$$

Comparing Equivalent Fractions with Same Numerators and Different Denominators

When fractions have the same numerator but different denominators, the denominators can be compared to determine the size of the fractions.

Note: The more equal parts a whole is divided into, the smaller the fraction.

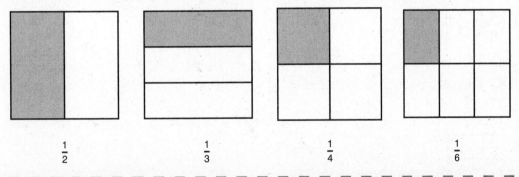

$$\frac{1}{2} \qquad\qquad \frac{1}{3} \qquad\qquad \frac{1}{4} \qquad\qquad \frac{1}{6}$$

NOTE

You can only compare fractions with the same size units. For example, $\frac{1}{2}$ and $\frac{2}{4}$ are not the same if the unit that is divided is not the same area.

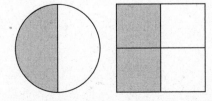

Comparing Fractions Practice Problems

(Answers can be found on pages 240–241.)

1. $\frac{3}{4}$ ☐ $\frac{1}{4}$

  ○ A. >
  ○ B. <
  ○ C. =

2. $\frac{1}{4}$ ☐ $\frac{2}{4}$

  ○ A. >
  ○ B. <
  ○ C. =

3. $\frac{2}{6}$ ☐ $\frac{1}{6}$

  ○ A. >
  ○ B. <
  ○ C. =

4. $\frac{4}{8}$ ☐ $\frac{4}{4}$

  ○ A. >
  ○ B. <
  ○ C. =

5. $\frac{3}{6}$ ☐ $\frac{4}{6}$

  ○ A. >
  ○ B. <
  ○ C. =

6. $\frac{3}{4}$ ☐ $\frac{1}{2}$

  ○ A. >
  ○ B. <
  ○ C. =

7. Michael ate $\dfrac{3}{4}$ of a Hershey bar, and his friend Chris ate $\dfrac{1}{4}$. Who ate more chocolate?

    O A.   Michael

    O B.   Chris

8. Shera ran $\dfrac{3}{4}$ of a mile. Scott ran $\dfrac{2}{8}$ of a mile. Who ran further?

    O A.   Shera

    O B.   Scott

9. Order the following fractions on the number line.

$$\dfrac{1}{4}, \dfrac{1}{2}, \dfrac{1}{1}$$

10. Order the following fractions from least to greatest on the number line.

$$\dfrac{1}{3}, \dfrac{3}{1}, \dfrac{2}{3}$$

Number and Operations—Fractions Chapter Review

(Answers can be found on pages 241–243.)

1. Which **three** models represent $\frac{1}{4}$?

   □ A.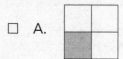

   □ B.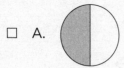

   □ C.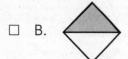

   □ D.

2. Which **two** models represent $\frac{1}{2}$?

   □ A.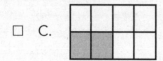

   □ B.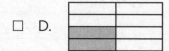

   □ C.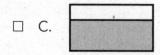

   □ D.

3. Which model represents $\frac{1}{3}$?

○ A.

○ B.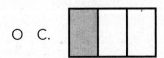

○ C.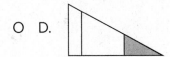

○ D.

4. There are five cookies. One is a peanut butter cookie and the rest are chocolate chip. What fraction of the total cookies does the peanut butter cookie represent?

○ A. $\frac{1}{5}$

○ B. $\frac{4}{5}$

○ C. $\frac{5}{5}$

○ D. $\frac{5}{1}$

5. Show where $\frac{2}{3}$ is located on the number line.

6. Mary baked twelve cupcakes. She gave four cupcakes to her friend. What fraction of the total cupcakes did she give to her friend?

    ○ A. $\frac{1}{2}$

    ○ B. $\frac{1}{3}$

    ○ C. $\frac{1}{4}$

    ○ D. $\frac{1}{6}$

7. Represent the number 4 as a fraction.

    ○ A. $\frac{1}{4}$

    ○ B. $\frac{4}{1}$

    ○ C. $\frac{4}{0}$

    ○ D. $1\frac{1}{4}$

8. $\frac{3}{4}$ ☐ $\frac{2}{4}$

    ○ A. >
    ○ B. <
    ○ C. =

9. $\frac{1}{4}$ ☐ $\frac{3}{4}$

    ○ A. >
    ○ B. <
    ○ C. =

10. $\dfrac{4}{6}\ \square\ \dfrac{3}{6}$

O A. >

O B. <

O C. =

11. Label the following number line with the fractions below:

$$\frac{3}{3},\ \frac{1}{3},\ \frac{9}{3},\ \frac{2}{3}$$

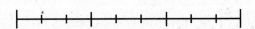

12. Malia ate $\dfrac{3}{4}$ of a sandwich, and her friend Jackson ate $\dfrac{1}{2}$. Who ate more

of the sandwich?

O A. Malia

O B. Jackson

13. Shera rode $\dfrac{3}{4}$ of a mile on her scooter. Amy rode $\dfrac{3}{8}$ of a mile. Who rode their

scooter further?

O A. Shera

O B. Amy

14. Order the following fractions on the number line.

$$\frac{1}{4},\ \frac{1}{2},\ \frac{1}{1},\ \frac{3}{4}$$

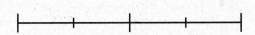

15. Order the following fractions from least to greatest.

$$\frac{1}{3},\ \frac{3}{1},\ \frac{2}{3},\ \frac{1}{6}$$

16. Using the model below, show how $\frac{2}{3}$ and $\frac{4}{6}$ are equivalent.

17. If Anthony ate $\frac{2}{6}$ of a pizza, how many slices does he have left?

 ○ A. 2

 ○ B. 6

 ○ C. 1

 ○ D. 4

18. Which fraction represents the number 5?

 ○ A. $\frac{5}{0}$

 ○ B. $\frac{1}{5}$

 ○ C. $\frac{5}{2}$

 ○ D. $\frac{5}{1}$

19. Which fraction is closest to $\frac{3}{4}$?

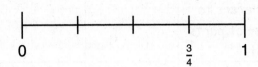

- O A. $\frac{1}{6}$

- O B. $\frac{2}{8}$

- O C. $\frac{1}{2}$

- O D. $\frac{1}{8}$

20. What area of the fraction is shaded?

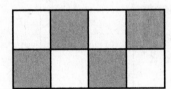

- O A. $\frac{1}{4}$

- O B. $\frac{1}{2}$

- O C. $\frac{4}{6}$

- O D. $\frac{3}{4}$

Progress Checklist

Fractions	Needs work	Working on	Mastered
The numerator refers to a specific number of parts of the whole unit.			
The denominator refers to the number of equal parts the whole is divided into.			
A fraction represents a number on a number line. It represents the distance between 0 and 1. You represent a fraction by dividing the number line into equal parts and specifying the length of the fraction. For example, $\frac{1}{2}$ represents one segment of a whole unit that is divided into 2 equal parts.			
Identify Units > Continuous (units that can be partitioned by cutting) > Discrete (units that can be partitioned by sorting)			
Partitioning Cutting or sorting units to equal parts			
Equivalence Fractions that are the same size			

Progress Checklist (continued)

Fractions	Needs work	Working on	Mastered
Models to Represent Fractions > Set (example: Marbles) > Area (example: Pizza) > Number lines			
Expressing Whole Numbers as Fractions E.g., $\frac{5}{1}$			
Equivalent Fractions			
Comparing Fractions with the Same Denominators $\frac{3}{4}, \frac{4}{4}, \frac{5}{4}$			
Compare Fractions with the Same Numerators E.g., $\frac{1}{2}, \frac{1}{3}, \frac{1}{4}$			
Comparing Fractions >, <, =			

Measurement and Data

Telling Time: Analog and Digital Clocks

Time is measured in hours, minutes, and seconds. The time between 12 (midnight) and 11:59 (in the morning) is called A.M. The time between 12 in the afternoon and 11:59 at night is called P.M. You can measure time using an **analog** clock or a **digital** clock. The difference between these clocks is that the analog clock shows how many minutes it is from the hour, and the digital clock tells you the exact time.

Analog Clock

An **analog clock** has numbers from 1 to 12 and one long hand and one short hand. The short hand is also called the hour hand. The **short hand** tells you what **hour** it is. The **long hand** tells you how many **minutes** have passed the hour. There are 60 minutes in one hour. Each number on the clock represents 5 minutes, so you can figure out how many minutes passed the hour by looking at the long hand.

The clock below shows the short hand is just passed 1. So the hour is 1. The long hand is pointing to the number 3. This means that 15 minutes have passed the hour. The time is 1:15 (one hour and fifteen minutes).

When the long hand is pointing at 12, you only need to look at the short hand to tell the time. In the example below, the short hand is pointing at the 2, and the long hand is on the 12. The time is 2:00.

Time (Analog Clock) Practice Problems

(Answers can be found on page 244.)

1. What time does the clock show? ....

2. What time does the clock show? ....

3. What time does the clock show? ....

4. What time does the clock show? ....

Digital Clocks

A digital clock is easier to read because it shows the exact hour and minutes. The number on the left side of the colon (:) shows the hour, and the numbers on the right side of the colon shows the minutes. Look at the clock below. The number on the left of the colon is 9. This means it is 9:00. The number on the right of the colon is 24. This means it is 24 minutes past the 9:00 hour. Notice that the clock also says A.M. on the right-hand side. This means the time is 9:24 A.M., so it is morning.

Addition and Subtraction of Time in Minutes

You can add or subtract time. There are 60 minutes in 1 hour. When adding time, if the minutes add up to 60 minutes, you add an hour to the time. If they add up to less than 60 minutes, then the hour does not change, only the minutes do. For example, if the time is 1:45, and you add 15 minutes, the minutes (45 + 15 = 60) add up to an hour, so the time will be 2:00. If you add 45 minutes and 20 minutes, you will have 65 minutes, or 1 hour and 5 minutes. If you add 15 minutes to 1:15, the time will be 1:30. In this case, only the minutes change and the hour does not.

You can figure out how much time has passed or how much time something will take by first adding the minutes together and then adding the hours together. If the minutes add up to less than 60, the hour does not change. If the minutes add up to 60 minutes or more, the hour changes.

Addition and Subtraction of Time in Minutes Practice Problems

(Answers can be found on page 244.)

1. Julia was getting ready for school. She finished eating breakfast at 6:30. When she finished eating, she packed up her things for school. When she looked at the clock, it said 6:47. How long did it take for Julia to pack up her things for school?

   O A. 47 minutes
   O B. 17 minutes
   O C. 3 minutes
   O D. 40 minutes

2. Heather is baking a cake. She put the cake in the oven at 5:00 P.M. The recipe said that she needs to bake it for 30 minutes. At what time should she take the cake out of the oven?

   O A. 5:30 P.M.
   O B. 5:00 P.M.
   O C. 45 minutes
   O D. 35 minutes

3. Scott is taking a test. He is given 45 minutes to complete the test. If he started the test at 10:20, what time will he finish the test?

    ○ A.   10:45
    ○ B.   11:05
    ○ C.   11:45
    ○ D.   10:54

4. Toniann played the piano for 20 minutes. If she started at 4:20, what time did she finish?

    ○ A.   4:40
    ○ B.   4:35
    ○ C.   3:40
    ○ D.   6:20

5. Craig and Lauren went on a hiking trip. They left the house at 8:00 A.M. It took them 2 hours and 30 minutes to hike the trail. When they were done hiking, they stopped at a restaurant for lunch. This took 1 hour and 15 minutes. What was the time on the clock when they finished their lunch?

    ○ A.   10:30
    ○ B.   11:45
    ○ C.   2:30
    ○ D.   3:45

Measure and Estimate Liquid Volume and Mass (Grams, Kilograms, and Liters)

If you go to the store, you will find that items such as orange juice, milk, soda, and water are sold in liters. Measuring the volume of liquids involves figuring out how much space the liquid takes up in the container. There are different units you can use to measure liquids. In third grade, you will know how to measure liquids using liters (l). The letter l is used to represent liters. A sports drink or a water bottle is usually about one liter. One liter is made up of 1,000 milliliters. Take a look at the picture below.

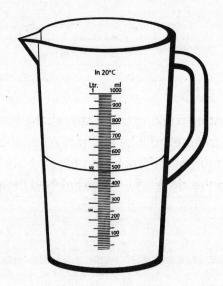

To figure out the quantity of liquid in the measuring cup above, you need to look at the scale. The left-hand side of this measuring cup shows the liters (l). The right-hand side shows the milliliters (ml). The line shows how much liquid is in the measuring cup. To figure out how much liquid is in the measuring cup, you have to read the scale.

In the measuring cup above, it shows the level of liquid as either $\frac{1}{2}$ of a liter or 500 milliliters.

Liquid Volume Measure Practice Problems

(Answers can be found on pages 244–245.)

1. The measuring cup holds one liter. How much liquid is in the measuring cup? Give your answers in liters (l) and milliliters (ml).

Answer .... liters .... milliliters

2. The measuring cup holds one liter. How much liquid is in the measuring cup? Give your answers in liters (l) and milliliters (ml).

Answer .... liters .... milliliters

3. A water bottle holds one liter of water. How much water is there in 2 water bottles?

Answer .... liters

4. A water bottle holds one liter of water. How many liters of water do $2\frac{1}{2}$ bottles hold?

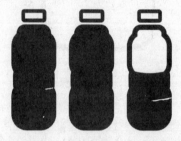

Answer .... liters

5. If the pitcher below holds one liter of water, draw a line to show how much $\frac{1}{2}$ a liter of water would look like.

6. If the pitcher below holds one liter of water, draw a line to show how much $\frac{1}{4}$ a liter of water would look like.

Mass Measure

Mass is the amount of matter in an object. The heavier an object, the more mass it has. You can use different units to measure mass. In third grade, you should know the difference between grams and kilograms. A kilogram is about 2.2 pounds. You need to be able to decide when it makes sense to use grams, and when it makes sense to use kilograms. You should be able to do the following:

Balance Weights

You can combine different units to equal the same weight.

For example, 1 kg = 500 grams + 500 grams.

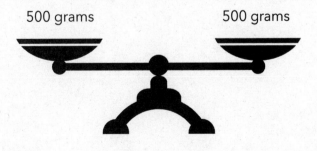

1 Kilogram = 1,000 grams

Adding and Subtracting Weight

You can add 40 kg and 4 kg to get 44 kg.

If you subtract 50 kg from 100 kg, you get 50 kg.

Comparing Weight

Which is heavier? Which is lighter? How much heavier?

35 pound dog

70 pound dog

Mass Measure Practice Problems

(Answers can be found on pages 245–246.)

1. Five bags of rice weigh one kilogram all together. How many grams does each bag of rice weigh?

    O   A.   5
    O   B.   20
    O   C.   200
    O   D.   150

2. Two bags of sugar weigh one kilogram. How many grams does each bag of sugar weigh?

    O   A.   500 grams
    O   B.   21 grams
    O   C.   2 grams
    O   D.   250 grams

3. Pam puts a 20-gram weight on a pan balance. How many 1-gram weights does she need to balance the scale to 20 grams?

    O   A.   20
    O   B.   5
    O   C.   21
    O   D.   10

4. Cole puts a 100-gram weight on a pan balance. How many 10-gram weights does he need to balance the scale to 100 grams?

    O   A.   25
    O   B.   20
    O   C.   110
    O   D.   10

5. Which of the items below would you measure in kilograms?

○ A.

○ B.

○ C.

○ D.

Geometric Measurement Data: Measure Length (with Rulers $\frac{1}{4}$ and $\frac{1}{2}$ Inch)

A ruler is used to measure **length**. This means you are measuring how long something is. The units that are used to measure length with a ruler are inches or feet. There are 12 inches in one foot. Look at the ruler below. One inch is the distance between 0 and 1. Two inches is the distance between 0 and 2. To measure the length of an object, place one end of the object you are measuring at 0 and figure out where the other end ends. The ruler below shows how 1 inch is divided into 4 equal parts. One of these four parts is $\frac{1}{4}$ of an inch. Two of these $\frac{1}{4}$ of an inch parts make up $\frac{1}{2}$ of an inch.

Measuring Length Practice Problems

(Answers can be found on page 246.)

1. Fill in the blanks using the ruler below.

A. 1 inch is equal to .... half inches.

B. 1 inch is equal to .... quarter inches.

C. 2 half inches is equal to .... quarter inches.

D. 3 inches is equal to .... half inches.

2. Max says his book measures 10 half inches. Mary disagrees and says it measures 5 inches. Explain why the two measurements are the same. Use words, pictures, or numbers.

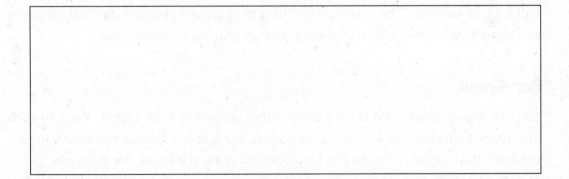

3. How many inches long is the pencil? ....

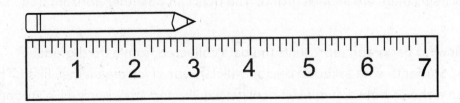

4. How many inches long is the pencil?

Data Analysis

You can look at trends and patterns in data to figure out answers to questions. This will help you make an informed choice. For example, you have to decide what flavor ice cream to bring to your class party. You want to make sure most of your classmates like the flavor you choose. You can use **data analysis** to make your decision. You first need to think of a question to ask your classmates. You can ask them, "What is your favorite flavor of ice cream?" Then, you have to organize the information you collect (**data**) in a graph. This will make it easier to analyze the data and look for patterns. There are different kinds of graphs you can use. In third grade, you should be familiar with bar graphs, picture graphs, and line plots.

Bar Graph

You can organize data that can be divided into groups in a bar graph. You can show how many items there are in each category. A bar graph is helpful because you can compare the height of the bars to figure out what the data says. For example, you can figure out which group has the most or least amount of data by the length of the bars. To create a bar graph, you need to label one part of the graph with the groups. The other part of the graph needs to be labeled with numbers to indicate how many items there are in each group. The bars can be either horizontal or vertical.

The following bar graph represents the data collected from a third-grade classroom. Students were asked to decide which flavor of ice cream they liked. They were given a choice between mint, chocolate, vanilla, and strawberry. Five students chose mint, seven students chose chocolate, nine students chose vanilla, and one student chose strawberry. By organizing this data in a graph, it is easy to see which flavor is the most popular. Each flavor is labeled and a bar is drawn to show how many students like each item. The bottom labels show the flavors of ice cream. The labels down the left side show the number of students.

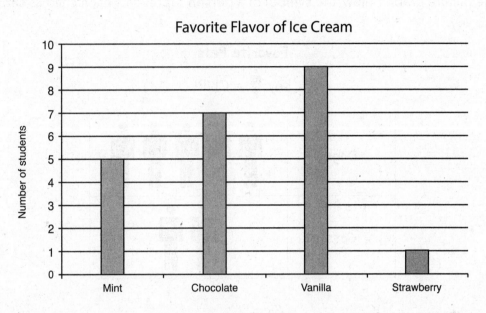

You can answer many questions by analyzing the bar graph. Below are some questions that you can answer based on the data in the bar graph above.

☐ What is the favorite flavor of ice cream?

Among those asked, nine students chose vanilla ice cream, so vanilla is the favorite flavor.

☐ What is the least favorite flavor of ice cream?

The least favorite flavor is strawberry, since only one student chose this flavor.

☐ How many more students liked chocolate ice cream than mint ice cream?

Seven students liked chocolate ice cream and five students liked mint ice cream, so 2 more students liked chocolate ice cream than mint ice cream.

Picture Graph

You can create a picture graph to organize your data. A picture graph shows how much there is in each category and uses a picture to represent a piece of data. From the graph, you can see that five children preferred dogs and two children liked cats. In the picture graph below, the symbol of a person represents each child as shown in the key.

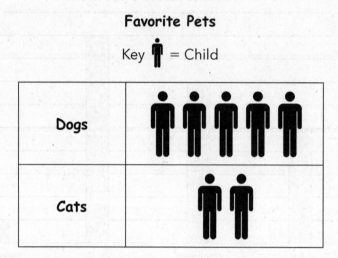

From this graph you can conclude that dogs are more popular than cats. You can also determine that three more children liked dogs over cats.

Line Plots

A line plot shows the frequency of data on a number line. The letter X is used to represent one piece of data on a number line. Line plots show how many pieces of data there are in each category.

The example below shows how many books each child read in a week.

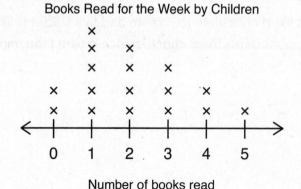

The X represents the number of children. The numbers on the number line represent the amount of books read. This graph shows that most children read one book during the week. There were two children who did not read any books. The most books read for the week were five.

A line plot can also be used to show categories of data. The line plot below tells you each child's favorite sport.

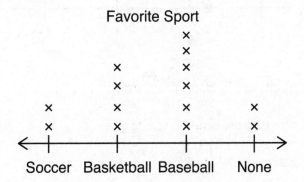

The bottom part shows the types of sports. In other words, it represents a category of things. The X represents one piece of data, in this case a child. From the data, you can see that four children liked basketball, and two children liked soccer. You can also create a line plot that has a scale that includes fractions.

Line Plot Practice Problems

(Answers can be found on pages 246–247.)

1. A company that makes gloves decided to collect data on the measurement of the lengths of hands of 15 people. The following data was collected. Make a line plot to organize the data.

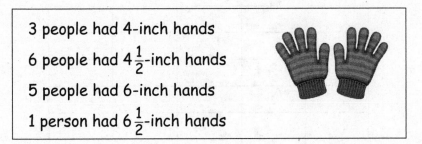

3 people had 4-inch hands

6 people had $4\frac{1}{2}$-inch hands

5 people had 6-inch hands

1 person had $6\frac{1}{2}$-inch hands

2. Hannah planted a garden and measured how much each plant grew. The graph below shows how many inches the plants grew.

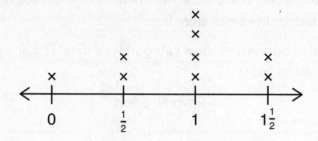

A. How many plants are in Hannah's garden? _____

B. How many plants grew one inch? _____

C. How many plants grew $\frac{1}{2}$ inch? _____

D. How many more plants grew 1 inch than $1\frac{1}{2}$ inches? _____

3. The table below shows how many of each color of M&Ms are in a bag. Create a picture graph to represent the data. Make sure you label your graph.

Color of M&M	Number of M&Ms
Red	4
Yellow	6
Green	2
Blue	5

How many more yellow M&Ms are there than red M&Ms? _____

Perimeter and Area

Perimeter

The perimeter is the distance around the shape. It is the sum of all the side lengths.

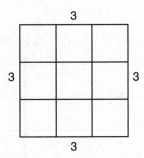

Perimeter = 3 + 3 + 3 + 3 = 12

Area

The area is the measure of a flat shape in square units. You can find the area of a rectangle by multiplying the number of square units in a row by the number of rows. The shape above is made up of $3 \times 3 = 9$ square units. Each square inside the square represents **1 square unit**. This square is made up of 9 square units. Depending on the size of the square, you can use different units to measure, such as square centimeters, square meters, square inches, and square feet.

NOTE

To measure the area of square units, it is important to place the squares inside so they touch each other without overlapping.

Unit

Area is measured in square units. For example, below is a 2×2 shape. Each square is one unit.

A shape can have different perimeters and areas.

You can figure out the area of a rectangle by breaking it down into easier problems. You can break the larger rectangle 3 × 7 into 3 × 5 and 3 × 2 to calculate the area.

$$3 \times 5 = 15 \text{ and } 3 \times 2 = 6$$

$$15 + 6 = 21$$

Area = 21 square units

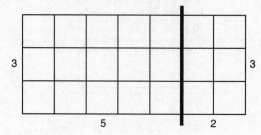

Perimeter and Area Practice Problems

(Answers can be found on pages 247–248.)

1. The rectangle below has a perimeter of 16 feet. Figure out the unknown side marked x, if the rest of the side lengths are known.

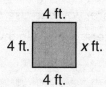

- O A. 12
- O B. 8
- O C. 4
- O D. 24

2. The rectangle below has a perimeter of 30 feet. Figure out the unknown side marked A, if the rest of the side lengths are known.

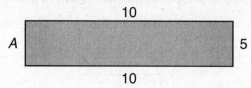

- O A. 5
- O B. 15
- O C. 20
- O D. 25

3. The school built a fence around the playground that had the shape below. The perimeter of the fence is 25 feet. Find the unknown side length marked Y.

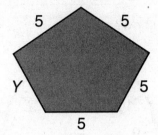

O A. 5
O B. 10
O C. 15
O D. 20

4. The figure below is made by joining two rectangles. What is the area?

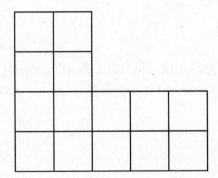

O A. 16 square units
O B. 25 square units
O C. 10 square units
O D. 14 square units

5. Draw two different shaped rectangles that each have an area of 8 square units.

Measurement and Data Chapter Review

(Answers can be found on pages 248–249.)

1. What time does the clock show?

    O A. 7:30

    O B. 6:40

    O C. 8:30

    O D. 6:40

2. Ed was getting ready for work. He started eating breakfast at 7:15 A.M. When he finished his breakfast it was 7:31. How long did it take Ed to eat his breakfast?

    O A. 31 minutes

    O B. 16 minutes

    O C. 46 minutes

    O D. 15 minutes

3. Ms. Lakey poured 3 1-liter water bottles into a fish tank. She added 10 more 1-liter water bottles to the fish tank. How much water did Ms. Lakey put into the fish tank?

    O A. 12 liters

    O B. 13 liters

    O C. 7 liters

    O D. 23 liters

4. Five bags of flour weigh one kilogram all altogether. How many grams does each bag of flour weigh?

- ○ A. 5
- ○ B. 20
- ○ C. 200
- ○ D. 150

5. What is the length of the pencil?

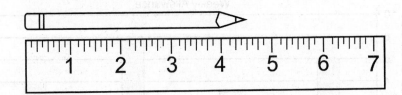

- ○ A. $1\frac{1}{2}$
- ○ B. $2\frac{1}{2}$
- ○ C. $3\frac{1}{2}$
- ○ D. $4\frac{1}{2}$

6. Which of the following items would you measure in kilograms?

○ A.

○ C.

○ B.

○ D.

7. Four bags of chocolate chips weigh one kilogram all together. How many grams does each bag of chocolate chips weigh?

- ○ A. 500 grams
- ○ B. 21 grams
- ○ C. 2 grams
- ○ D. 250 grams

8. Use the bar graph below to answer the questions that follow.

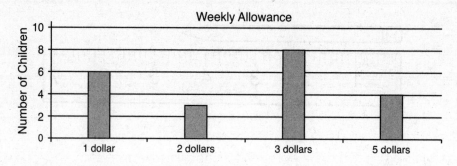

A. How many children earned $3 a week? _____

B. How many more children got $3 instead of $5? _____

9. Use the picture graph below to answer the questions that follow.

Favorite Food

Key 👤 = Child

Pizza	👤 👤 👤 👤 👤
Hot dogs	👤 👤

A. How many children like pizza? _____

B. How many children like hot dogs? _____

C. How many more children like pizza than hot dogs? _____

10. Use the line plot below to answer the questions that follow.

Height of Third-Grade Students in Inches

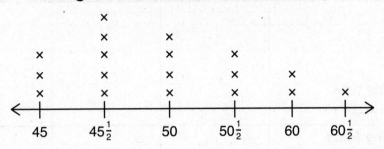

A. How many third graders are $45\frac{1}{2}$ inches tall? ....

B. How many third graders are taller than $50\frac{1}{2}$ inches? ....

11. The rectangle below has a perimeter of 32 feet. Figure out the unknown side length marked x, if the rest of the side lengths are known.

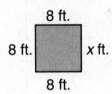

8 ft.

8 ft. x ft.

8 ft.

O   A.   12
O   B.   8
O   C.   4
O   D.   24

12. The figure below is made by joining two rectangles. What is the area?

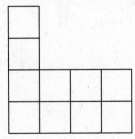

O   A.   16 square units
O   B.   25 square units
O   C.   10 square units
O   D.   14 square units

Progress Checklist

	Needs work	Working On	Mastered
Time Digital Analog Measuring time Elapsed time			
Measuring Mass Grams Kilograms **Measuring Volume** Liters **Measuring Length** Inches $\frac{1}{4}$, $\frac{1}{2}$ **Adding and Subtracting Mass/Volume** Balancing weights Adding and subtracting weights/liquids Estimation			
Graphs Line plot Bar graph Picture graph			
Area Area models (rectangles) Compose and decompose regions to find area of shapes. **Perimeter**			

Geometry

Geometric Shapes and Figures

In third grade, you should be able to look at a shape and figure out what group it belongs to by looking at its properties.

Right Angle

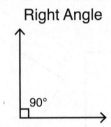

A right angle has an interior angle of 90 degrees. For example, a corner of a square or rectangle is a right angle. It is made up of two perpendicular lines.

Parallel Lines

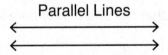

Parallel lines are two lines that never touch. They are the same distance apart.

Quadrilaterals

A quadrilateral is a four-sided shape. There are different types of quadrilaterals. Squares, rectangles, rhombuses, trapezoids, and parallelograms are all quadrilaterals.

Types of Quadrilaterals

Parallelograms

A parallelogram is a four-sided shape. Parallelograms have two pairs of parallel sides. The angles opposite each other are equal.

Rectangles

Rectangles have four right angles and two parallel sides. The sides opposite each other are equal.

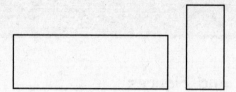

Squares

A square has four sides that have the same length and four right angles. It has two pairs of parallel sides.

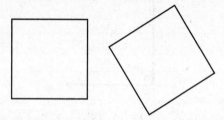

Trapezoids

A trapezoid is a quadrilateral that has one pair of parallel sides

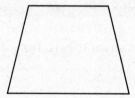

Rhombus

A rhombus is a parallelogram with four equal length sides. The angles opposite each other are equal.

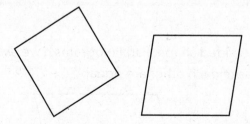

Geometry Practice Problems

(Answers can be found on pages 249–250.)

1. Which **three** shapes are quadrilaterals?

   □ A.

   □ B.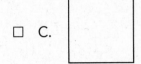

   □ C.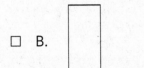

   □ D.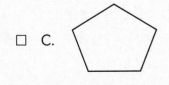

2. Which **two** shapes are rectangles?

   □ A.

   □ B.

   □ C.

   □ D.

3. Which of the following shapes is a square?

O A.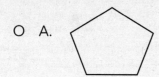

O B.

O C.

O D.

4. Which of the following shapes has four right angles?

O A.

O B.

O C.

O D.

5. Which **two** shapes are trapezoids?

□ A.

□ B.

□ C.

□ D.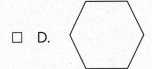

6. Which **three** shapes are rhombuses?

□ A.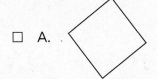

□ B.

□ C.

□ D.

7. Which of the following shapes is a parallelogram?

O   A.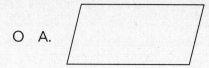

O   B.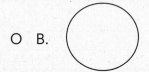

O   C.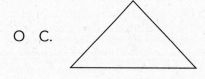

O   D.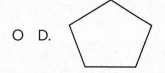

8. Which **two** shapes have four right angles?

☐   A.   Square
☐   B.   Rectangle
☐   C.   Circle
☐   D.   Triangle

9. Which **two** shapes have parallel lines?

☐   A.   Square
☐   B.   Rectangle
☐   C.   Circle
☐   D.   Triangle

10. Which of the following shapes has four sides and only one pair of parallel lines?

O   A.   Square
O   B.   Rectangle
O   C.   Trapezoid
O   D.   Triangle

Congruent and Similar Shapes

Congruence

Shapes are congruent if they have equal length sides and angles that have equal measures. If the shapes are congruent, you will be able to put one shape over the other, and it will be exactly the same shape and size. This is important to know if you are cutting a whole into equal size pieces that are the same shape.

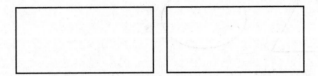

Similar

Shapes are similar if they have congruent angles and their sides are the same. It is the same shape but a different size. The shapes below are similar. They have the same shape but not the same size.

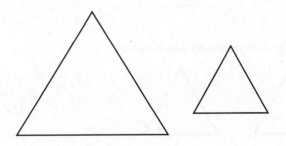

Congruent and Similar Shapes Practice Problems

(Answers can be found on page 250.)

1. Which of the following shapes are congruent?

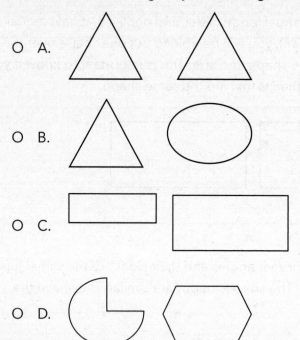

O A.

O B.

O C.

O D.

2. Which of the following shapes are similar?

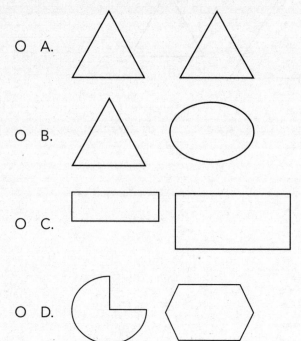

O A.

O B.

O C.

O D.

Partitioning

Partitioning is another word for splitting a whole into pieces. You can split a whole into equal size pieces. The pieces are equal if they are the same size pieces. For example, you can split a square into four equal pieces. Each part of the square is $\frac{1}{4}$ of the whole.

$\frac{1}{4}$	$\frac{1}{4}$
$\frac{1}{4}$	$\frac{1}{4}$

Partitioning Practice Problems

(Answers can be found on page 250.)

1. Which **two** of the following shaded parts of the circles represent half of the circle?

   ☐ A.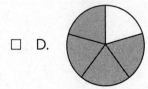

   ☐ B.

   ☐ C.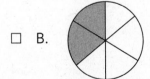

   ☐ D.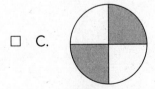

2. What fraction of the whole is shaded?

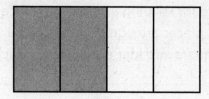

- ○ A. $\dfrac{1}{4}$

- ○ B. $\dfrac{1}{3}$

- ○ C. $\dfrac{1}{2}$

- ○ D. $\dfrac{3}{4}$

3. Which picture shows $\dfrac{1}{3}$ of the whole shaded?

- ○ A.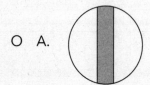

- ○ B.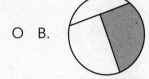

- ○ C.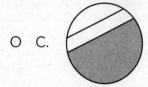

- ○ D.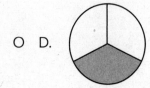

Geometry Chapter Review

(Answers can be found on pages 250–251.)

1. Which **two** shapes are quadrilaterals?

☐ A.

☐ B.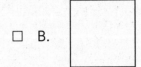

☐ C.

☐ D.

2. Which **three** shapes have right angles?

☐ A.

☐ B.

☐ C.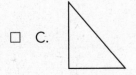

☐ D.

3. Which **two** shapes are parallelograms?

☐ A.

☐ B.

☐ C.

☐ D.

4. Which **two** shapes have four right angles?

☐ A. Octagon
☐ B. Rectangle
☐ C. Circle
☐ D. Square

5. Which of the following shapes are congruent?

O A.

O B.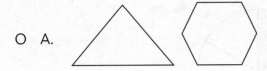

O C.

O D.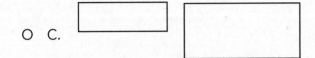

6. Which of the following shapes are similar?

O A.

O B.

O C.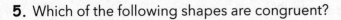

O D.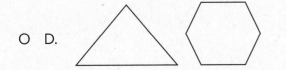

7. What fraction of the whole is shaded?

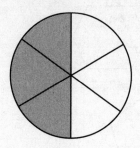

    ○ A. $\frac{1}{3}$

    ○ B. $\frac{1}{2}$

    ○ C. $\frac{3}{4}$

    ○ D. $\frac{1}{4}$

8. Which **two** of the following shaded parts represent half of a square?

☐ A.

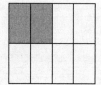

☐ B.

☐ C.

☐ D.

9. Which of the following shapes is a trapezoid?

O A.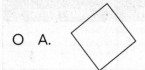

O B.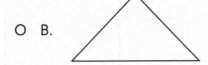

O C.

O D.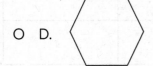

10. Which **two** shapes are rhombuses?

☐ A.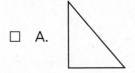

☐ B.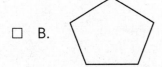

☐ C.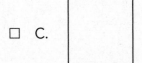

☐ D.

Progress Checklist

	Needs Work	Working on	Mastered
Right angles Parallel lines			
Quadrilaterals Rectangle Rhombus Square Trapezoid Parallelogram			
Similar Congruent Equal area			
Connect shapes to fractions			

Math Practice Test

(Answers can be found on pages 251–258.)

1. An orange has a mass of 25 grams. An apple has a mass that is 100 grams more than the orange. What is the mass of the apple in grams?

   O A.   100 grams
   O B.   25 grams
   O C.   75 grams
   O D.   125 grams

2. Does replacing the unknown number with 6 make the equation true?
   Select **YES** or **NO** for each equation.

	YES	NO
$5 \times \square = 5$		
$6 \times \square = 64$		
$36 \div \square = 36$		
$42 \div \square = 7$		

3. The school playground is in the shape of a rectangle. The playground is 70 feet wide and 40 feet long. Calculate the perimeter of the park.

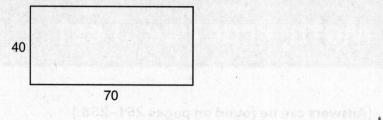

- ○ A. 220
- ○ B. 110
- ○ C. 210
- ○ D. 400

4. Which **two** shapes are quadrilaterals?

☐ A.

☐ B.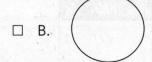

☐ C.

☐ D.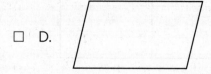

5. Which one of the following shapes is also a rhombus?

- ○ A. Square
- ○ B. Rectangle
- ○ C. Circle
- ○ D. Pentagon

6. Students voted on their favorite color. Use the bar graph below to answer the question that follows.

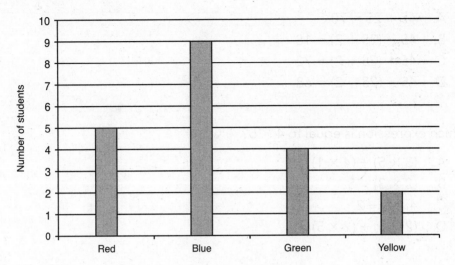

How many more students chose blue than yellow? ....

7. Use the number line below to solve the problem that follows.

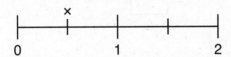

Choose the number line that shows a number equal to the point shown by point X on the number line above.

○ A.

○ B.

○ C.

○ D

8. Gabby has $45. She buys a toy for $25 and an ice cream cone for $2. Which equation shows how much money Gabby will have left?

    O A.   45 + 25 = 70

    O B.   45 − (25 + 2) = 18

    O C.   45 + (25 + 2) = 72

    O D.   45 + (25 − 2) = 68

9. Which expression is equal to 4 × 5?

    O A.   (3 × 5) + (4 × 1)

    O B.   (2 × 3) − 5

    O C.   4 × 5 − 2

    O D.   (2 × 5) + (2 × 5)

10. The figure below is made by joining two rectangles. What is the area, in square feet, of the figure?

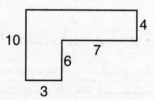

    O A.   58 square feet

    O B.   50 square feet

    O C.   72 square feet

    O D.   86 square feet

11. Which equation has the same unknown value as 48 ÷ 8 = ?

    O A.   8 ÷ 48 = ☐

    O B.   8 × ☐ = 48

    O C.   48 × ☐ = 8

    O D.   ☐ ÷ 8 = 48

12. Which unknown numbers complete the pattern on the number line?

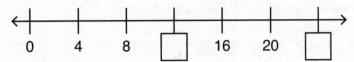

- O A. 12, 24
- O B. 10, 24
- O C. 12, 26
- O D. 14, 25

13. Maria has 24 Hershey Kisses. She equally divides the Hershey Kisses and gives them to 6 children. How many Hershey Kisses does each child get?

- O A. 3
- O B. 4
- O C. 5
- O D. 6

14. Place each fraction below in their correct location on the number line.

$$\frac{3}{3}, \frac{1}{3}, \frac{4}{3}$$

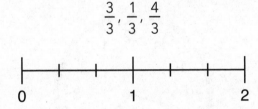

15. When you compare two fractions that both have a numerator of 1, the fraction with the bigger denominator is larger? **TRUE** or **FALSE**?

16. Label the number line with the following fractions.

$$\frac{1}{2}, \frac{1}{3}, \frac{1}{6}$$

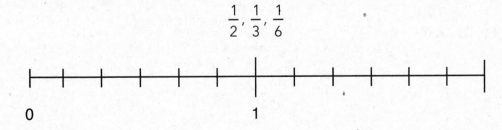

17. Thomas drew a polygon with a perimeter of 30 units. He covered the area of the polygon with tiles that are 1 square unit each.

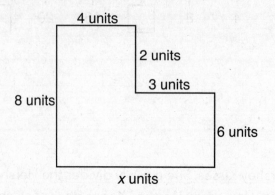

What equation could be used to find the value of x? ....

How many tiles did Thomas use to cover the polygon? ....

18. Use the clock to answer the question. What is the time, to the nearest minute, shown on the clock?

○ A. 4:40
○ B. 8:21
○ C. 1:21
○ D. 8:05

19. A parking lot has cars parked in 4 rows. There are 5 cars in each row. How many cars are parked in the parking lot?

○ A. 15
○ B. 45
○ C. 9
○ D. 20

20. Decide if each equation is true or false. Check either **TRUE** or **FALSE** for each equation.

	TRUE	FALSE
$3 \times 8 = 24 + 2$		
$4 \times 5 = 20 \div 5$		
$3 \times 4 = 24 \div 2$		

21. Shade $\frac{1}{4}$ of the whole.

22. Which unknown number makes this equation true?

$7 \times \boxed{} = 35$

○ A. 4
○ B. 5
○ C. 6
○ D. 7

23. Craig placed the pencil on top of the ruler as shown below. What is the length of the pencil in inches?

- ○ A. $1\frac{1}{2}$ inches

- ○ B. $2\frac{1}{2}$ inches

- ○ C. $2\frac{1}{4}$ inches

- ○ D. $1\frac{3}{4}$ inches

24. Shera has 6 erasers. She estimates that the total mass of the erasers is 24 grams. Which statement could Shera use to make her estimate?

- ○ A. Each eraser has a mass of about 4 grams.
- ○ B. Each eraser has a mass of about 6 grams.
- ○ C. Three erasers have a mass of 20 grams.
- ○ D. Three erasers have a mass of 18 grams.

25. What unknown number makes this equation true?

$756 - 245 = \boxed{}$

- ○ A. 500
- ○ B. 511
- ○ C. 250
- ○ D. 325

26. Joey has 4 stacks of quarters. Ben has 6 stacks of quarters. Each stack of quarters is worth $10. How much more money, in dollars, does Ben have than Joey?

    O A. $20
    O B. $30
    O C. $40
    O D. $50

27. Mary has 3 pies. Each pie is cut into 6 pieces. Mary eats 2 pieces. Which equation shows how many pieces are left?

    O A. $(6 \times 3) + 2$
    O B. $(3 - 6) + 2$
    O C. $(3 + 6) + 2$
    O D. $(3 \times 6) - 2$

28. A brownie has a mass of 24 grams. A juice box has a mass that is 92 grams more than the brownie. What is the mass of the juice box in grams?

    O A. 116 grams
    O B. 92 grams
    O C. 87 grams
    O D. 125 grams

29. Does replacing the unknown number with 4 make the equations true? Select **YES** or **NO** for each equation.

	YES	NO
$3 \times \square = 6$		
$6 \times \square = 24$		
$32 \div \square = 8$		
$42 \div \square = 7$		

30. The school playground is in the shape of a rectangle. The playground is 35 feet wide and 60 feet long. Calculate the perimeter of the playground.

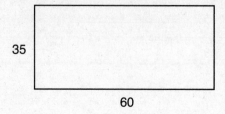

35

60

○ A. 95
○ B. 190
○ C. 155
○ D. 200

31. Which **two** shapes are quadrilaterals?

☐ A.

☐ B.

☐ C.

☐ D.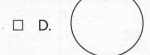

32. Students voted on their favorite pet. Use the bar graph below to answer the question that follows.

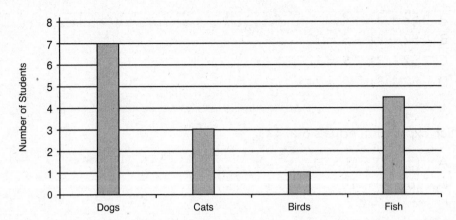

How many more students chose dogs over cats? ....

33. Which shape is also a rhombus?

   ○ A.   Pentagon
   ○ B.   Square
   ○ C.   Triangle
   ○ D.   Circle

34. Use the number line below to solve the problem that follows.

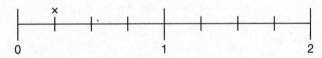

Choose two number lines that show a number equal to the point shown by point x on the number line above.

   ☐ A.

   ☐ B.

   ☐ C.

   ☐ D

35. Tina had $52 to spend. She bought a pair of shoes for $31 and a pocket book for $9. Which equation shows how much money Tina has left?

- O A. $52 + 31 = 83$
- O B. $52 - 31 + 9 = 30$
- O C. $52 - 31 - 9 = 12$
- O D. $52 + 31 - 9 = 74$

36. Which expression equals 6×4?

- O A. $(3 \times 2) + (3 \times 1)$
- O B. $(6 \times 4) - 10$
- O C. $4 \times 6 - 4$
- O D. $(6 \times 2) + (6 \times 2)$

37. The figure below is made by joining two rectangles. What is the area, in square feet, of the figure?

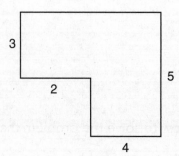

- O A.   26 square feet
- O B.   14 square feet
- O C.   35 square feet
- O D.   42 square feet

38. Which equation has the same unknown value as $32 \div 4 = \Box$?

- O A. $4 \div 32 = \Box$
- O B. $4 \times \Box = 32$
- O C. $31 \times \Box = 8$
- O D. $\Box \div 4 = 8$

39. Which two numbers complete the pattern on the number line?

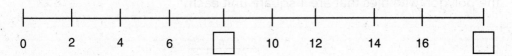

- O A. 12, 14
- O B. 9, 17
- O C. 8, 18
- O D. 7, 19

40. Ann has 36 gummy bears. She divides the gummy bears equally and gives them to 6 children. How many gummy bears does each child get?

- O A. 3
- O B. 4
- O C. 5
- O D. 6

41. Write each fraction below in their correct location on the number line.

$$\frac{2}{3}, \frac{1}{3}, \frac{5}{3}$$

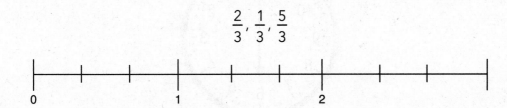

42. When you compare two fractions that each has a numerator of 1, the fraction with the smaller denominator is larger? **TRUE** or **FALSE**?

43. Place the following fractions in their correct location on the number line.

$$\frac{1}{3}, \frac{1}{2}, \frac{1}{6}$$

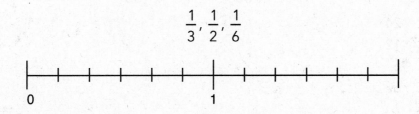

44. Hannah drew a polygon with a perimeter of 20 units. She covered the area of the polygon with tiles that are 1 square unit each.

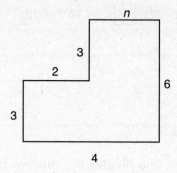

What is the value of n? _____

45. Use the clock to answer the question. What is the time, to the nearest minute, shown on the clock?

- ○ A. 2:30
- ○ B. 6:00
- ○ C. 6:50
- ○ D. 1:20

46. An egg carton has 2 rows of 6 eggs. How many eggs are in the carton?

- ○ A. 24
- ○ B. 12
- ○ C. 6
- ○ D. 62

47. Decide if each equation is true or false. Check either **TRUE** or **FALSE** for each equation.

	TRUE	FALSE
2 × 8 = 16 + 2		
4 × 5 = 2 × 10		
2 × 4 = 16 ÷ 2		

48. Shade $\frac{1}{3}$ of the whole.

49. Jeremy placed the paperclip on top of the ruler as shown below. What is the length of the paperclip in inches?

○ A. $1\frac{1}{2}$ inches

○ B. $2\frac{1}{2}$ inches

○ C. $2\frac{1}{4}$ inches

○ D. $1\frac{3}{4}$ inches

50. Which unknown number makes the equation true?

$5 \times \boxed{} = 25$

- O A. 4
- O B. 5
- O C. 6
- O D. 7

51. Liz has 4 bagels. She estimates that the total mass of the bagels is 20 grams. Which statement could Liz use to make her estimate?

- O A. Each bagel has a mass of about 5 grams.
- O B. Each bagel has a mass of about 6 grams.
- O C. Three bagels have a mass of 15 grams.
- O D. Three bagels have a mass of 16 grams.

52. What unknown number makes this equation true?

$325 - 145 = \boxed{}$

- O A. 440
- O B. 175
- O C. 180
- O D. 125

53. Noelle has 5 stacks of quarters. Angela has 8 stacks of quarters. Each stack of quarters is worth $10. How much more money, in dollars, does Angela have than Noelle?

- O A. $10
- O B. $20
- O C. $30
- O D. $40

54. Miguel has 4 pizzas. Each pizza is cut into 8 slices. Miguel eats 4 slices. How many slices are left? Which **two** equations show how many slices are left?

- ☐ A. $(4 \times 8) - 4$
- ☐ B. $(8 - 4) + 2$
- ☐ C. 4×7
- ☐ D. $(4 \times 8) - 2$

CHAPTER 15

Math Answers Explained

Chapter 9: Operations and Algebraic Thinking

Answers for Multiplication Practice Problems (pages 88–91)

1. **A** There are 3 dogs. Each dog eats 5 bones. This means that there are 3 groups of 5 bones. It is the same as $5 + 5 + 5$. You can write it as a multiplication problem of 3×5. This means that there are 3 groups of 5 bones.

2. **C** Keisha wanted to buy 5 tickets. Each ticket costs $6. To figure out how much money she needs to buy 5 tickets, you must multiply 5 by 6. This is the same as $6 + 6 + 6 + 6 + 6$. You can write it as a multiplication problem of 5×6. The answer is 30 because $5 \times 6 = 30$.

3. **A** There are 6 children. Each child gets 3 cookies. To figure out the total number of cookies, you have to multiply 6×3. Three groups of six cookies is $6 \times 3 = 18$.

4. **C** There are 5 notebooks. Each notebook gets 2 stickers. This means there are 5 groups each with 2 stickers. This can be written as 5×2.

5. **D** There are 7 boxes of chocolate. Each box contains 8 chocolate bars. To figure out the total amount of chocolate bars, you have to add 7 together 8 times. This can be written as a multiplication sentence of 7×8. Seven groups of 8 is 56: $7 \times 8 = 56$.

6. **A** $9 \times 3 = 27$

7. **C** $4 \times 5 = 20$

8. **C** $8 \times 3 = 24$

9. **A** $6 \times 6 = 36$

10. **A** You can use the distributive property. 4 can be split into $2 + 2$. Multiply $(2 \times 7) + (2 \times 7)$.

11. **D** Marcy has 4 stacks of quarters. If each stack is worth $2, you have to multiply $4 \times \$2$ to figure out how much money Marcy has. Marcy has $8. Jim has

9 stacks of quarters. Each stack is worth $2. So you have to multiply 9 × $2 to figure out how much money Jim has. He has $18. To figure out how much more money Jim has than Marcy, you have to subtract $18 − $8. Jim has $10 more than Marcy.

12. **B** 3 × 8 represents 3 groups of 8.

13. **C** The array is made up of two groups of 8. You can write it as 2 × 8.

14. **D** You can use the associative property. The 7 can be broken down to the more friendly numbers of 5 and 2. Then, you can multiply the 5 and the 2 by 7 and add the answers together

$$(7 \times 2) + (7 \times 5)$$
$$14 \quad + \quad 35 = 49$$

15. **D** If you skip count by adding 4, the missing number will be 12.

16. **C** A rectangular table has a length of 10 feet and a width of 6 feet. To find the area, you have to multiply the length times the width. 10 × 6 = 60. The area equals 60 square feet.

Answers for Division Practice Problems (pages 94–96)

1. **D** The total amount of apples is 25. Five people share them equally. To figure out how many apples each person gets, you have to split the 25 apples into 5 equal groups. If you divide 25 apples into 5 equal groups, there will be 5 apples in each group. There are a couple of ways you can divide.

Drawing a picture

You can also use your multiplication facts: 5 × 5 = 25 and 25 ÷ 5 = 5.

2. **A** There are 16 cookies in all. If two children share them equally, you have to divide the 16 cookies into 2 equal groups. There are a couple of ways to solve this problem:

Drawing a picture

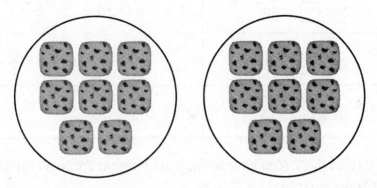

You can also use your multiplication facts: $2 \times 8 = 16$ and $16 \div 2 = 8$. Or you can add $8 + 8 = 16$.

3. **C** Zack has $20. He wants to buy tickets. We know that each ticket costs $4. What we want to know is how many $4 tickets Zack can buy with $20. To do this, we have to divide $20 by $4. There are a couple of ways to solve this. You can use your multiplication facts: $4 \times 5 = 20$, or you can also divide. You know that there are 5 groups of four in 20, so $20 \div 4 = 5$. Another way is to skip count: 4, 8, 12, 16, 20. You have to skip count 5 times to get to 20 when starting at 4.

4. **B** There are 28 pennies. If you divide 28 into 7 equal groups, you will have 4 pennies in each group: $28 \div 7 = 4$. You can also use the multiplication facts $7 \times 4 = 28$ to figure out the answer. You can also skip count 7, 14, 21, 28. You have to skip count 4 times to get to 28.

5. **C** There are 30 hot dogs. Each child eats 2 hot dogs. We need to figure out how many children ate 2 hot dogs. In other words, we need to know how many groups of 2 are in 30. There are 15 groups of 2 in 30, so $30 \div 2 = 15$. Another way is to skip count by 2s 15 times.

6. **C** Ms. Jane has a total of 21 books. She gives each child 3 books. In order to figure out how many children got books, you have to divide 21 books by 3. You are figuring out how many groups of 3 there are in 21. You can use your multiplication fact 3×7 to figure out that there are 7 groups of 3 in 21. This means $21 \div 3 = 7$. You can also skip count by 3s 7 times.

7.

	YES	NO
$6 \times \square = 36$	✔ $6 \times 6 = 36$	
$5 \times \square = 30$	✔ $5 \times 6 = 30$	
$64 \div \square = 8$		✔ $64 \div 6 \neq 8$
$60 \div \square = 10$	✔ $60 \div 6 = 10$	

8. **C** 18 divided by 9 is 2. You have to plug the number 2 into all the equations to see which ones are true. $12 \times 2 = 24$

9.

	TRUE	FALSE
$2 \times 5 = 5 \div 2$		✔
$3 \times 8 = 48 \div 2$	✔ $3 \times 8 = 24$ $48 \div 2 = 24$	
$10 \times 3 = 25 \div 5$		✔

10. **B** This is because $4 \times 7 = 28$.

Answers for Two-Step Word Practice Problems (pages 98–100)

1. **A** The problem says that Latisha has some marbles. This means that the number of Latisha's marbles is unknown. The letter *m* is used to show how many marbles Latisha has. You have to add Latisha's marbles and Jose's marbles together to get 45 marbles. This is represented by the equation $m + 26 = 45$.

2. **C** The total amount of money Jen had was $45. She gave $25 to her brother and brought a T-shirt for $7. The problem is asking how much money does Jen have left. In order to figure this out, you have to subtract the $25 she gave her brother and the $7 she spent for the T-shirt from $45, which is the total amount of money she had.

$45 − $25 = $20 (money she had left after she gave her brother $25)

$20 − $7 = $13 (money she had left after giving her brother $25 and
spending $7 on a T-shirt)

3. The total amount of money the class made is $48.

    Cost of 10 cupcakes at $2 $10 × $2 = 20
    Cost of 8 sodas at $1 $8 × $1 = 8
    Cost of 4 pies at $5 $4 × $5 = 20

    Total amount spent: $20 + $8 + $20 = $48

4. You can use any letter to represent the missing value. In this example, the letter
    x is used to represent the missing value.

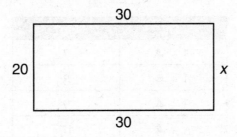

    To find the missing value, you have to add the sides. The total perimeter is 100.

    $$20 + 30 + 30 + x = 100$$
    $$80 + x = 100$$
    $$100 − 80 = 20$$
    $$x = 20$$

    Another way to think about this problem is to subtract the sides from 100 to
    figure out what is left. $100 − 20 − 30 − 30 = 20$.

5. Cameron has 58 cars left. Cameron had 120 Hot Wheels cars. He gave half to
    his sister and two to his friend. You have to figure out how many Cameron
    has left.

    When Cameron gives half to his sister, he has 60 left: $120 − 60 = 60$.
    After Cameron gives 2 cars to his friend, he has 58 left: $60 − 2 = 58$.

Answers for Arithmetic Pattern Practice Problems (pages 103–104)

1. **B** 1, 11, 21, 31, 41, <u>51</u>—Each number in the pattern increases by 10.

2. **D** 3, 6, <u>9</u>, 12, 15—You skip count by 3. Each number in the pattern increases
    by 3.

3. **C** 44, 42, 40, 38, <u>36</u>—The rule is subtract 2. Each number in the pattern decreases by 2.

4. **B** If you add 2 to these numbers, it makes up the sequence. You can try adding 2 to the numbers in the pattern and see if it works. Let's look at choice A. If you add 2 to 3, the next number should be 5. But it says six. So you know that this does not work.

5. **C** The rule is add 4 because if you add 4 to the In number, it matches the Out number.

Rule
+4

In	Out
3 + **4**	7
4 + **4**	8
5 + **4**	9
6 + **4**	10

6. **A** If you multiply 6 by 2, it is 12.

Rule
× 2

In	Out
2 × 2	4
4 × 2	8
6 × 2	**12**
8 × 2	16

Answers for Operations and Algebraic Thinking Chapter Review (pages 105–109)

1. **A** Christopher wants to buy 3 packs of Pokémon cards. Each pack costs $7. Christopher wants to know how much money he needs. He will need to multiply the number of packs of cards by the cost of each pack of cards. 3 × $7 = $21.

2. **B** There are 4 childen. Each child eats 2 lollipops. The problem is asking for the total amount of lollipops the childen ate. We need to figure out what 4 groups of 2 is: $2 + 2 + 2 + 2 = 8$. This problem can be easier written as a multiplication problem: $4 \times 2 = 8$.

3. **A** $9 \times 3 = 27$

4. **D** The expression 5×8 can be broken down to smaller problems. The 8 is made into a more friendly number of 5 and 3. You can break up the number by multiplying them separately and then adding the products together. You can use the distributive property:

$$(5 \times 3) + (5 \times 5)$$
$$15 \ + \ \ 25 = 40$$

5. **B** $6 + 6 + 6$ is the same as 3×6 (3 groups of 6).

6. **A** The array is 4×3.

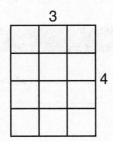

7. **B** There is a total of 24 strawberries. The 24 strawberries need to be split equally into 8 groups because 8 people are sharing them. You can write it as $24 \div 8 = 3$. You can draw 8 circles to represent the number of people and divide the 24 strawberries equally into 8 groups. You can also use your multiplication facts to help you figure out how many 8s are in 24: $8 \times 3 = 24$. You know that there are 3 eights in 24. You can also skip count 3 times to figure out how many 8s are in 24. For example, 8, 16, 24 (you had to skip count 3 times).

8. **B** There are 16 ounces of sugar. Each batch of cookies uses 4 ounces of sugar. The problem is asking you to figure out how many 4 ounce batches of sugar there are in 16 ounces of sugar. To do this, you need to divide 16 by 4. There are several strategies you can use. You can use your multiplication facts. Four goes into 16 four times. Another strategy you could use is to keep subtracting 4 from 16. You have to subtract 4 four times.

$$16 - 4 = 12$$
$$12 - 4 = 8$$
$$8 - 4 = 4$$
$$4 - 4 = 0$$

9. You need to substitute the box with 4 and work out the problem to see if it makes sense.

	YES	NO
$6 \times \square = 24$	✔ $6 \times 4 = 24$	
$5 \times \square = 30$		✔ $5 \times 4 \neq 30$
$14 \div \square = 8$		✔ $14 \div 4 \neq 8$
$60 \div \square = 10$		✔ $60 \div 4 \neq 10$

10. You need to calculate both sides and see if they are equal.

	True	False
$3 \times 5 = 15 + 0$	✔ $15 = 15$	
$4 \times 2 = 16 \div 2$	✔ $8 = 8$	
$10 \times 4 = 25 \div 5$		✔ $40 \neq 5$

11. **A** Bob has some gumballs. We don't know how many gumballs he has. So let's use the variable m to represent the gumballs. We know that Juan has 6 gumballs. Together, they have 21 gumballs. $m + 6 = 21$.

12. **D** 5, 10, 15, 20, 25, <u>30</u>—Add 5 to each number.

13. **A** 7, 14, 21, <u>28</u>, 35—Add 7 to each number.

14. **A** Skip count by 3s.

15. **C** Add 4 to each In number.

In	Out
4 + **4**	8
5 + **4**	9
6 + **4**	10
7 + **4**	11

Chapter 10: Number and Operations in Base 10

Answers for Whole Number Place Value Practice Problems (pages 112–113)

1. **A** It represents 8 one units. (It is in the ones place.)

2. **B** It represents 7 ten units.

3. **A** It has 1 ten unit and 2 one units that make up 12 units: 10 + 2 = 12.

4. **B** It represents 241. It is made up of 200 + 40 + 1 (2 hundred units, 4 ten units, and 1 one unit).

5. **C** The numbers add up to 125: 100 + 20 + 5 = 125.

Answers for Rounding to the Nearest 10 or 0 Practice Problems (pages 114–115)

1. **A** The number is 5 or more, so round up to 10.

2. **B** The number is less than 5, so round down to 0.

3. **A** The number is 5 or more, so round up to 10.

4. **B** The number is less than 5, so round down to 0.

5. **A** The number is 5 or more, so round up to 10.

Answers for Rounding to the Nearest 10 Practice Problems (page 116)

1. **B** The digit 5 in 35 should be rounded up. The nearest 10 is 40.

2. **A** The digit 6 in the number 76 is greater than 5. Round up to the nearest 10, which would be 80.

3. **A** The digit 8 in the number 28 is greater than 5. Round up to the nearest 10, which would be 30.

4. **C** The digit 4 in the number 84 is less than 5. Round down to the nearest 10. This would be 80.

5. **C** The digit 2 in the number 32 is less than 5. Round down to the nearest 10. This would be 30.

Answers for Rounding to the Nearest 100 Practice Problems (page 118)

1. **A** The 59 in the number 259 is greater than 50. Round up to 300.

2. **C** The 62 in the number 762 is greater than 50. Round up to 800.

3. **A** The 23 in the number 923 is less than 50. Round down to 900.

4. **A** The 55 in the number 555 is greater than 50. Round up to 600.

5. **C** The 42 in the number 942 is less than 50. Round down to 900.

Answers for Addition Practice Problems (pages 123–124)

1. **B** The numbers 20 and 30 can be thought of as 2 groups of ten and 3 groups of ten, which makes 5 groups of ten. This equals 50. You can also use the algorithm 20 + 30.

$$20 + 30 = 50$$

2. **A** There are several ways the problem can be solved. You can make friendly numbers and add them: 50 + 10 + 4. You can combine the 50 + 10 and get 60 and then add 4. Or, you can add the 0 and 4 and get 4, and then add the tens together of 5 + 1 and get 6 tens, which represents 60. Then add the columns and get 64.

$$
\begin{array}{r}
50 \\
+ \ 14 \\
\hline
64
\end{array}
$$

3. **D** The numbers 60 + 20 can be combined together to get 80. The numbers 7 and 2 can be added together to get 9. If you add 80 plus 9, you get 89.

4. **B** 74 + 23 + 15 = 112. There are several ways this problem can be solved. One way is to use the associate property. This means you can combine two numbers and then add the rest. 74 + 23 equals 97. Then you can add 97 + 15 to get 112. Or, you can add the numbers in the ones place 4 + 3 + 5 and get 12. Then, you can add the numbers in the tens place 70 + 20 + 10 = 100. Lastly, add 100 + 12 = 112.

5. **C** 14 + 9 + 74 = 97. The numbers 14 + 9 can be added together to make 23, and then 23 + 74 can be added together to make 97. You can also add the numbers in the ones place. 4 + 9 + 4 can be added together to make 17, and the numbers in the tens place 10 + 70 can be added together to make 80. Lastly, add 80 + 17 = 97.

6. **B** 20 + ? = 37. This is a Change Unknown problem. You have to figure out the missing number. There are two ways to think about this problem. 20 plus what makes 37? You can think about how much more you need to get to 37. Another way is to think about subtraction. You can subtract 20 from 37 to get 17.

7. **D** ? + 15 = 27. This is a Start Unknown problem. You have to figure out the missing number. You can count up from 15 to 27 and get 12. Or, you can subtract 27 − 15 to get the answer.

8. **A** This is a Join problem. 26 + 25 = 51.

9. **C** ? + 22 = 46. This is a Start Unknown problem. You can subtract 22 from 46. 46 − 22 = 24. Or, you can count up from 22 to 46 and get 24.

10. **B** $22 + $27 = $49. This is a Join problem.

Answers for Subtraction Practice Problems (page 126)

1. **B** You have to subtract 15 from 45. 45 − 15 = 30.

2. **C** 31 − ? = 15. You can subtract 15 from 31 to figure out how many pies were sold. Or, you can count down from 31 until you reach 15 to figure out how many pies were sold. 31 − 15 = 16.

3. **B** ? − $12 = $15. If $15 was left, then you have to add $12 to $15 to figure out the total amount of money Savanah had, which is $27.

Answers for Groups of 10 Practice Problems (page 128)

1. **A** 2 groups of 30 is 60.

2. **C** 5 groups of 20 is 100.

3. **A** 7 groups of 20 is 140.

4. **C** 3 groups of 10 is 30.

5. **C** 4 groups of 20 is 80.

Answers for Number and Operations in Base 10 Chapter Review (pages 129–132)

1. **A** 6 ones units. The six is in the ones place.

2. **D** Five 100 units. It is in the hundreds place.

3. **A** There are 3 tens and 2 ones, which makes a total of 32.

4. **A** There is $80 + 9$ in 89.

5. **A** You have to round up for numbers 5 or greater.

6. **A** You have to round down for numbers less than 50.

7. **D** $45 + 26 = 71$. There are several strategies you can use. You can add $40 + 20$ and get 60, and add $5 + 6 = 11$, and then add them together, $60 + 11 = 71$. You can also use the standard algorithm:

$$\begin{array}{r} {}^{1}45 \\ + \ 26 \\ \hline 71 \end{array}$$

8. **A** $10 + 16 + 28 = 54$. You can add these numbers in many ways. One way is to combine the 10s together, $10 + 10 + 20 = 40$, and add the ones together $6 + 8 = 14$. Then, you can add $40 + 14 = 54$. Another way is to combine 10 and 16 to get 26, and then add that to 28. $26 + 28 = 54$. Find a strategy that is easy for you.

9. **C** Mary had 15 paperclips. She was given some more. We don't know how many more paperclips she was given. $15 + ? = 27$. You can count up to 27 or subtract 15 from 27 to get the answer.

10. **A** $4 \times 10 = 40$

11. **B** $32 - 5 = 27$

12. **C** The pet store had 42 hamsters. They sold some hamsters. We don't know how many hamsters they sold. We do know they have 12 left. $42 - ? = 12$, $42 - \mathbf{30} = 12$. You can figure this out by subtracting 30 from 42 or counting up from 12 to 42.

13. **A** $? - 7 = 19$. You can add 7 to the 19 to figure out the total amount of bags of chips that Scott had.

14. **B** $? + 9 = 67$. You can also subtract 9 from 67 to find the answer.

15. **C** You have to add 17 and 58 to get the total.

Chapter 11: Number and Operations—Fractions

Answers for Identifying Fractions Practice Problems (pages 141–143)

1. **A and B** These two models have been partitioned into two equal parts. One of the parts is shaded representing $\frac{1}{2}$.

2. **C** If there are four pies and one is a blueberry and the rest are apple, then three out of the four pies are apple. This means $\frac{3}{4}$ of the total pies are apple pies.

3. **A** The orange is split into six equal pieces, and one piece was eaten, so there are 5 pieces left. $6 - 1 = 5$. The five pieces represent $\frac{5}{6}$ of the whole.

4. **A and B** Choice A is a set model. The whole is made up of six objects. Two of them represent $\frac{1}{3}$ of the whole. Choice B is a linear model. The whole has been split into three equal segments. One of these represents $\frac{1}{3}$.

5. The number line should be divided into fourths or four equal pieces. $\frac{3}{4}$ represents three of the four pieces. It is the distance from zero to $\frac{3}{4}$ on the number line.

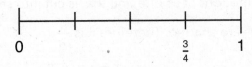

6. **C** She will have seven slices left if she started out with eight and ate one.

7. **B**. The whole is made up of two tacos. One taco represents one out of two tacos and makes up $\frac{1}{2}$ the total tacos.

8. **C** The answer is $\frac{2}{4}$. The cake is cut into four pieces. Two pieces would represent two out of the four pieces, which is $\frac{2}{4}$ of the total cake.

9. **C** Three out of six represents $\frac{3}{6}$ of the total.

10. Note: The whole unit is the rectangle. The rectangle has been divided into different size pieces. It might be helpful to draw out the pieces to identify the parts.

$\frac{1}{4}$	$\frac{1}{8}$	$\frac{1}{8}$
$\frac{1}{2}$		

Answers for Expressing Whole Numbers as Fractions Practice Problems (pages 146–148)

1. **B and D** Choice B is a linear model. The unit of one is divided into three equal parts. $\frac{4}{3}$ would be $1\frac{1}{3}$. Choice D is an area model. It represents one whole and an additional $\frac{1}{3}$, which makes $\frac{4}{3}$.

2. Each longer line represents a whole unit.

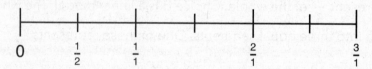

3. **A and B** If the two circles are considered two different units, then the shaded parts represent one whole circle and an additional $\frac{1}{3}$ from the other. The two circles can also be thought of as one unit that is cut into six equal pieces. Four out of the six pieces are shaded. Therefore it is $\frac{4}{6}$.

4. **B** The whole number five can be represented as $\frac{5}{1}$. The numerator, 5, represents the total number of parts. The denominator is 1. It represents the whole unit. This means that there are five parts in the whole unit.

5. **B** The numerator is 6. This represents that the whole is divided into 6 parts. The denominator is one, which represents the whole.

6. The number line can be labeled as whole numbers divided by one.

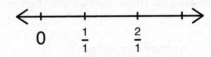

$$0 \qquad \frac{1}{1} \qquad \frac{2}{1}$$

7. **A and B** It can be represented as $\frac{2}{1}$, which is the same as 2 or $\frac{4}{2}$. If four is divided into two equal parts, there will be two parts in each group.

8. **B and D** It can be represented as $\frac{4}{1}$, which represents four. It can also be represented by $\frac{8}{2}$. If eight is divided into two equal parts, there will be four in each group.

Answers for Equivalent Fractions Practice Problems (pages 150–152)

1. **A, B, and C** The models in choices A and C are divided into four equal parts, and one part is shaded. This represents $\frac{1}{4}$ of the whole. The model in choice A is a linear model. The whole has been divided into four equal segments. The model in choice B is an equivalent faction to $\frac{1}{4}$. It is an area model. It is divided into eight equal pieces, and two are shaded. Two $\frac{1}{8}$ pieces is equivalent to $\frac{1}{4}$. The model in choice C is an area model. The square is divided into four equal pieces. One piece represents $\frac{1}{4}$ of the whole.

2. The whole has been divided into four equal parts. Therefore, if you divide the four into two equal groups, it would represent half of the fraction. Another way to think about this problem is $\frac{2}{4}$ is equivalent to $\frac{1}{2}$ because it has the same area.

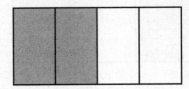

3. The whole has been divided into six equal parts. If you divide the six parts into three equal groups, then two parts will make up a $\frac{1}{3}$. Therefore, $\frac{2}{3}$ is made up of two $\frac{1}{3}$ parts. Another way to think about it is that $\frac{4}{6}$ is equivalent to $\frac{2}{3}$.

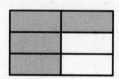

4. **C and D** $\frac{2}{4}$ and $\frac{3}{6}$ are equivalent. They have the same area as $\frac{1}{2}$.

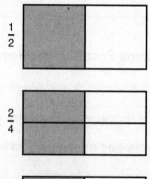

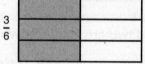

5. **True** They are equivalent. They have the same area.

6. **False** $\frac{4}{6}$ and $\frac{1}{3}$ do not have the same area.

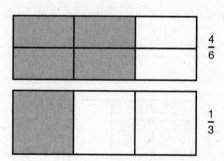

7. There are a couple of ways to show this. The model below is one way. The important point here is that the models show that they have the same area.

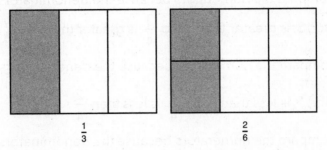

$$\frac{1}{3} \qquad \frac{2}{6}$$

8. There are a couple of ways to show this. The model below is one way. The important point here is that the models show that they have the same area.

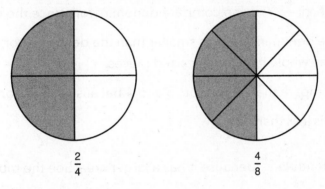

$$\frac{2}{4} \qquad \frac{4}{8}$$

9. **C** There are different ways the answer can be drawn. The drawing below shows one way. The main point is that both pictures show the same area.

One represents $\frac{1}{3}$ and the other represents $\frac{3}{9}$.

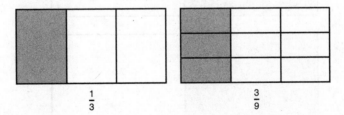

$$\frac{1}{3} \qquad \frac{3}{9}$$

10. **C** $\frac{1}{3}$ is equivalent to $\frac{2}{6}$.

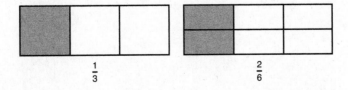

$$\frac{1}{3} \qquad \frac{2}{6}$$

Answers to Comparing Fractions Practice Problems (pages 154–155)

1. **A** You can compare the numerators because the denominators are the same. The numerator, 3, is greater than 1. So $\frac{3}{4}$ is greater than $\frac{1}{4}$.

2. **B** You can compare the numerators because the denominators are the same. The numerator, 1, is less than 2. So $\frac{1}{4}$ is less than $\frac{2}{4}$.

3. **A** You can compare the numerators because the denominators are the same. The numerator, 2, is greater than 1. So $\frac{2}{6}$ is greater than $\frac{1}{6}$.

4. **B** $\frac{4}{8}$ is less than $\frac{4}{4}$. You can compare denominators since the numerators are the same. The denominator, 8, is smaller than the denominator, 4, because you have to cut the whole into smaller sized pieces.

5. **B** You can compare the numerators 3 and 4 because the denominators are the same. So, $\frac{3}{6}$ is less than $\frac{4}{6}$.

6. **A** $\frac{3}{4}$ is greater than $\frac{1}{2}$ because it has a larger area. See the model below.

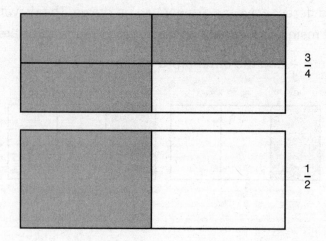

7. **A** You can compare the numerators since the denominators are the same. 3 is greater than 1. So $\frac{3}{4}$ is greater than $\frac{1}{4}$.

8. **A** You can use a linear model to compare the fractions.

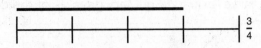

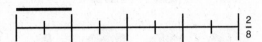

9.

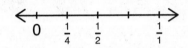

10.

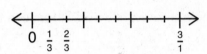

Answers for Number and Operations—Fractions Chapter Review (pages 156–161)

1. **A, C, and D** These three choices all have the same area and are equivalent fractions.

2. **A and B** The models in choices A and B are divided into two equal parts. Each part represents a half of the model.

3. **C** The rectangle is divided into three equal parts. The shaded part is one third of the whole rectangle.

4. **A** One out of the five cookies represents $\frac{1}{5}$. The numerator is 1 and the denominator is 5 since it makes up the whole batch of cookies.

5.

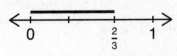

6. **B** Mary made twelve cupcakes. The total amount of cupcakes is twelve, and she gave four to a friend. The numerator is 4, so she gave $\frac{4}{12}$ of the cupcakes to

her friend. However, this is not in the answer. So you have to find an equivalent fraction. There are three 4s in 12. So, Mary gave $\frac{1}{3}$ of the cupcakes away.

7. **B** The whole number is 4 and the size of the unit is 1 whole. So it would be $\frac{4}{1}$.

8. **A** You can compare the numerators 3 and 2 because the denominators are the same. 3 is greater than 2. So, $\frac{3}{4} > \frac{2}{4}$.

9. **B** You can compare the numerators 1 and 3 since the denominators are the same. Therefore, $\frac{1}{4}$ is less than $\frac{3}{4}$.

10. **A** You can compare the numerators since the denominators are the same. 4 is great than 3, so $\frac{4}{6}$ is greater than $\frac{3}{6}$.

11.

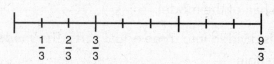

12. **A** $\frac{3}{4}$ is greater than $\frac{1}{2}$.

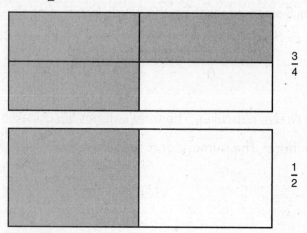

13. **A** You can compare the denominators since the numerators are the same. The denominator, 4, would result in a larger distance than an eighth of a mile.

14.

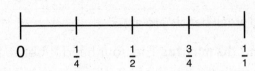

15. $\dfrac{1}{6}, \dfrac{1}{3}, \dfrac{2}{3}, \dfrac{3}{1}$

16. There is more than one way to draw a model. The picture below shows one way. The important point is to show that both models have the same area.

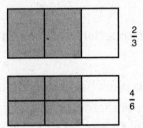

17. **D** Anthony would have to cut the pizza into six equal slices in order eat $\dfrac{2}{6}$ of the pizza. This means if he ate 2 slices, there will be 4 slices left. This would be $\dfrac{4}{6}$ of the pizza.

18. **D** If the whole number is 5, when you write it as a fraction, the denominator is 1 because it remains a whole unit.

19. **C** $\dfrac{1}{6}, \dfrac{2}{8}$, and $\dfrac{1}{8}$ are smaller than $\dfrac{1}{2}$. Therefore, $\dfrac{1}{2}$ is the closest number to $\dfrac{3}{4}$.

20. **B** Four out of the eight squares are shaded. This area is equivalent to $\dfrac{1}{2}$ of the fraction.

Chapter 12: Measurement and Data

Answers for Time (Analog Clock) Practice Problems (pages 166–167)

1. **12:00** The big and small hands are at 12.

2. **1:40 or 1 hour and 40 minutes** The hour hand is between 1 and 2. This means it is 1:00. The minute hand is at 8. This means it is at 40 minutes. The time is 1 hour and 40 minutes, or 1:40.

3. **10:15** The hour hand is at 10, and the minute hand is at 3, which means 15 minutes has passed the 10:00 hour. The time is 10:15.

4. **8:30** The hour hand is between 8 and 9. The minute hand is at 6. This means 30 minutes have passed the 8:00 hour. The time is 8:30.

Answers for Addition and Subtraction of Time in Minutes Practice Problems (pages 168–169)

1. **B** It took Julia 17 minutes to pack her things for school. You can count up from 30 to 47 minutes and figure out it took her 17 minutes. You can also subtract the time. (47 − 30 minutes is 17 minutes.) The hour stays the same, so you don't have to worry about the 6:00 hour since only minutes passed.

2. **A** Heather should take the cake out of the oven at 5:30. You need to add 30 minutes to 5:00. This would make it 5:30.

3. **B** Scott finished the test at 11:05. If you add 45 to 20 minutes, that would be a total of 65 minutes. This is 5 minutes more than an hour, so you need to add an hour plus 5 minutes. This means if Scott started the test at 10:20, it would be 5 minutes passed the next hour, which would make it 11:05.

4. **A** Toniann finished playing the piano at 4:40. It would be 4:40 because you add the 20 minutes she played the piano to the 20 minutes from the time on the clock.

5. **B** The time on the clock when they finished their lunch was 11:45. You have to add 2 hours and 30 minutes and 1 hour and 15 minutes. You can add the hours together and get 3 hours. The minutes add up to 45 minutes. If they started at 8 and you added 3 hours and 45 minutes, it would be 11:45.

Answers for Liquid Volume Measure Practice Problems (pages 171–173)

1. $\frac{1}{4}$ **liter and 250 milliliters** (read the line).

2. $\frac{1}{2}$ **liter and 500 milliliters** (read the line).

3. **2 liters** (add the 2 liters together).

4. **2$\frac{1}{2}$ liters** (add the 2$\frac{1}{2}$ liters together).

5. Draw a line half way.

6. Draw a line $\frac{1}{4}$ of the way. The whole is divided into 4 equal parts. $\frac{1}{4}$ is one of

those parts.

Answers for Mass Measure Practice Problems (pages 175–176)

1 **C** Since 1 kilogram is made up of 1,000 grams, you have to divide 1,000 by 5. This will be 200 grams.

2. **A** Since 1 kilogram is made up of 1,000 grams, you have to divide 1,000 by 2. This will make it 500 grams.

3. **A** Pam needs twenty 1-gram weights, 20 × 1 = 20. In other words, there are 20 one grams in a single 20-gram weight.

4. **D** Cole needs ten 10-gram weights because 10 × 10 = 100.

5. **B** A child is much heavier than the other items. Therefore, it makes sense to use the kilogram. 1 kilogram = 1,000 grams. A paper clip weighs about a gram.

Answers for Measuring Length Practice Problems (pages 177–178)

1. A. 1 inch is equal to 2 half inches.

   B. 1 inch is equal to 4 quarter inches.

   C. 2 half inches are equal to 4 quarter inches.

   D. 3 inches are equal to 6 half inches.

2. They are the same because 10 half inches is equal to 5 inches. There are 2 half inches in an inch, so 5 inches is made up of 10 half inches.

3. The pencil is 3 inches long.

4. The pencil is $2\frac{1}{2}$ inches long.

Answers for Line Plot Practice Problems (pages 181–182)

1.

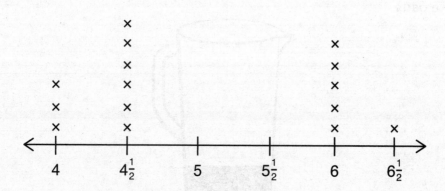

2. A. There are nine plants in Hannah's garden. You have to count the X's because each one represents a single plant.

   B. 4

   C. 2

   D. There are two more. There are four 1-inch plants and two $1\frac{1}{2}$-inch plants.

3.

Number of M&M colors

	M		
	M		M
M	M		M
M	M		M
M	M	M	M
M	M	M	M
Red	**Yellow**	**Green**	**Blue**

There are two more yellow M&Ms than there are red M&M's.

Answers for Perimeter and Area Practice Problems (pages 184–185)

1. **C** If the perimeter is 16, then the side lengths must add up to 16.

$$4 + 4 + 4 + x = 16$$

The unknown side length is 4.

2. **A** If the perimeter is 30, then the side lengths must add up to 30.

$$10 + 10 + 5 + A = 30$$

The missing number is 5.

3. **A** The perimeter is 25 feet. Y is 5 because the side lengths need to add up to 25.

$$5 + 5 + 5 + 5 + y = 25$$

4. **D** It is made up of 14 square units.

5. Here are some shapes you can make 1 × 8, 4 × 2, and 2 × 4.

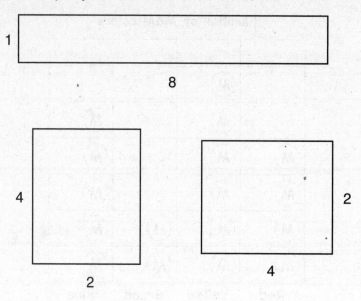

Answers for Measurement and Data Chapter Review (pages 186–189)

1. **C** It is 8:30. The hour hand is between the 8 and 9. The minute hand is at 6.

2. **B** If you count up from 15 to 31, it will be 16 minutes. You can also subtract 31 − 15 to get the answer.

3. **B** Ms. Lakey pours 13 liters into the fish tank. 3 liters + 10 liters = 13 liters

4. **C** You have to first convert the kilogram to grams. 1 kilogram is made up of 1,000 grams. 1,000 grams divided into 5 equal groups is 200 grams.

5. **D** The pencil is $4\frac{1}{2}$ inches long.

6. **B** The dog is heavier than the other items and weighs more than a kilogram.

7. **D** There are 1,000 grams in 1 kilogram. If you divide 1,000 into four equal groups, it will be 250 grams.

8. A. Eight children earned $3 a week.

   B. Four children got $5 and eight children got $3 dollars. This means four more children got $3 instead of $5 dollars.

9. A. There are five children who like pizza.

    B. There are two children who like hot dogs.

    C. There are three more children who like pizza than hot dogs.

10. A. Five third graders are $45\frac{1}{2}$ inches tall.

    B. Three third graders are taller than $50\frac{1}{2}$ inches. Two of these third graders are 60 inches and the other third grader is $60\frac{1}{2}$ inches.

11. **B** The perimeter is 32 feet. The sides should add up to 32 feet.

$$8 + 8 + 8 + x = 32 \text{ feet}$$

12. **C** There are 10 square units. You can count up the squares.

Chapter 13: Geometry

Answers for Geometry Practice Problems (pages 193–196)

1. **A, C, and D** A quadrilateral is a four-sided shape. Choice A is a rectangle. It has four sides. Choice B is a triangle. It has three sides, so it is not a quadrilateral. Choice C is a square, and it has four sides. This makes it a quadrilateral. Choice D has four sides, so it is a quadrilateral.

2. **A and B** These are both rectangles. They both have two parallel sides and four right angles.

3. **D** This is a square because it has four equal sides and four right angles.

4. **C** This shape has four right angles. The figure in choice D only has two right angles.

5. **A and B** These are trapezoids. They have two parallel lines, and are four-sided figures.

6. **A, B, and C** These shapes are rhombuses because they are parallelograms and have four equal length sides. The opposite angles are equal.

7. **A** This is a parallelogram. It is a four-sided shape. There are two pairs of parallel lines.

8. **A and B** These are a square and a rectangle and both have four right angles.

9. **A and B** These are a square and a rectangle and both have parallel lines.

10. **C** This is a trapezoid and has only one pair of parallel lines and four sides.

Answers for Congruent and Similar Shapes Practice Problems (page 198)

1. **A** The triangles are both congruent because they are the same size and the same shape.

2. **C** The rectangles are similar because they have the same shape but are different sizes.

Answers for Partitioning Practice Problems (pages 199–200)

1. **A and C** Choice A has one of the two parts shaded, so it represents half of the whole. The circle in choice C is split into four equal parts. Two of these parts make up $\frac{1}{2}$ of a circle, so it is an equivalent fraction. It represents half of the whole.

2. **C** The rectangle is split into four equal parts. Two of these parts are shaded. This represents half of the four pieces.

3. **D** Only choice D represents $\frac{1}{3}$ because it is $\frac{1}{3}$ of the whole. The whole is divided into three equal pieces.

Answers for Geometry Chapter Review (pages 201–205)

1. **A and B** A square and a rectangle are quadrilaterals.

2. **B, C, and D** These shapes all have right angles. A right angle has an interior angle of 90 degrees. It is made up of two perpendicular lines.

3. **A and D** These shapes have parallel lines that never touch.

4. **B and D** A square and a rectangle are made up of four right angles (90 degree angles).

5. **B** The pentagons are congruent because they have the same shape and size.

6. **B** The circles are similar because they have the same shape but not the same size. They are proportionally the same.

7. **B** Half of the circle is shaded. The circle is divided into six equal pieces. Three of the pieces are shaded, and they represent half of the circle.

8. **B and C** Exactly half of the whole square is shaded.

9. **C** A trapezoid has two parallel sides

10. **C and D** Both of these shapes are rhombuses. They have two sets of parallel lines.

Answers for Math Practice Test (pages 207–222)

1. **D** The orange is 25 grams. We know that the apple is 100 more grams than the orange. This means we have to add 100 grams and 25 grams.

$$100 + 25 = 125 \text{ grams}$$

2.

	YES	NO
$5 \times \square = 5$		✔ $5 \times 6 \neq 5$
$6 \times \square = 64$		✔ $6 \times 6 \neq 64$
$36 \div \square = 36$		✔ $36 \div 6 \neq 36$
$42 \div \square = 7$	✔ $42 \div 6 = 7$ 6×7 is 42	

3. **A** You have to add up the sides to find the perimeter. In a rectangle, opposite sides have the same length. So you have to add up $70 + 70 + 40 + 40 = 220$.

4. **C and D** Quadrilaterals are shapes that have four sides, and both a rectangle and a trapezoid have four sides.

5. **A** A square is also a rhombus. A rhombus is a flat shape with four equal straight sides. The opposite sides are also parallel. A square also has four equal sides.

6. Seven more students chose blue than yellow. Nine students chose blue and two students chose yellow.

$$9 - 2 = 7$$

7. **D** It is half of the whole. The whole is divided into thirds. However, in this case the markings do not help. In the example, the mark is halfway between 0 and 1 and represents half because the whole is divided into two equal segments. In

choice D, the whole is divided into three segments, so the halfway point is not indicated with a marking. It is between the first and second markings.

8. **B** The total is $45. To find out how much money is left, you must subtract $25 and $2 from the total amount of money.

$$\$45 - \$25 - \$2 = \$18$$

9. **D** You can use the distributive property to divide the 4 into two sets, and then multiply each part by 5.

$$(2 \times 5) + (2 \times 5)$$

$$10 \;+\; 10 = 20$$

10. **A** You can decompose the shape to create two rectangles. The lengths of opposite sides of a rectangle are the same. The area of one rectangle is $7 \times 4 = 28$. The area of the other rectangle is $10 \times 3 = 30$. You add these two numbers together to get the total area: $28 + 30 = 58$ square feet.

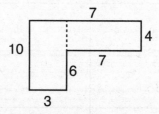

11. **B** This is correct because $8 \times 6 = 48$.

12. **A** The pattern increases by 4, so the numbers that fill in the missing numbers on the number line are 12 and 24.

13. **B** If Maria has 24 Hershey Kisses, and she divides them equally among 6 children, then each child will get 4 Hershey Kisses: $24 \div 6 = 4$. If you take 24 Hershey Kisses and divide them into 6 equal groups, there will be 4 in each group.

14. Each whole has been divided into three equal segments. The denominator is 3. The top part (numerator) indicates the number of thirds.

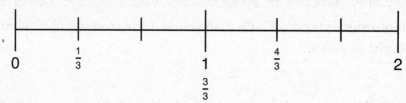

15. **False** The denominator is the number of equal parts the whole is divided into. The bigger the denominator, the smaller the part because it is cut into smaller sized pieces.

16. The number line is divided into sixths.

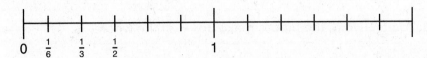

17. The value of $x = 4 + 3$. x is the same length as the 4 plus 3 units because opposite sides of a rectangle have the same length.

    The figure could be divided into two rectangles. The area of one rectangle is 4×8 units, and the area of the other rectangle is 3×6 units. $4 \times 8 = 32$ units and $3 \times 6 = 18$ units. You can then add these two numbers together to figure out the area of the whole figure: $32 + 18 = 50$ square units.

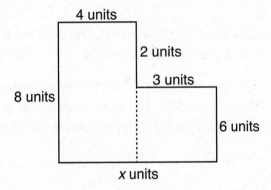

18. **B** The time is 8:21. The hour hand is at 8, and the minute hand is at one minute past the 4. This means that 21 minutes have passed.

19. **D** You have to multiply the number of rows by the number of parking spots in each row to find out how many cars are parked in the parking lot: $4 \times 5 = 20$.

20. Decide if each equation is true or false. Check either true or false for each equation.

	TRUE	FALSE
$3 \times 8 = 24 + 2$		✔ $24 \neq 26$
$4 \times 5 = 20 \div 5$		✔ $20 \neq 4$
$3 \times 4 = 24 \div 2$	✔ $12 = 12$	

21. The whole is divided into eight equal pieces. $\frac{1}{4}$ is the whole divided into four equal parts. Two of the pieces make up $\frac{1}{4}$ of the whole.

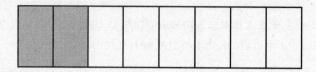

22. **B** The unknown number is 5. This is because $7 \times \mathbf{5} = 35$.

23. **A** The length of the pencil is $1\frac{1}{2}$ inches. It starts at 1 and ends at $2\frac{1}{2}$. This distance is $1\frac{1}{2}$ inches.

24. **A** Each eraser has a mass of about 4 grams. The total mass of all 6 erasers is 24 grams. If you divide 24 by 6, it is 4: $6 \times 4 = 24$.

25. **B** $756 - 245 = 511$. There are many different ways to solve this problem. You could take $700 - 200$ and get 500, and then subtract $56 - 45$ and get 11. $500 + 11 = 511$. Another way is by using the standard algorithm.

$$\begin{array}{r} 756 \\ -\ 245 \\ \hline 511 \end{array}$$

26. **A** Joey has 4 stacks of quarters. If each stack of quarters is worth $10, this means Joey has $10 \times 4 = $40. Ben has 6 stacks of quarters. It is worth $6 \times $10 = $60. To figure out how much more money Ben has, you can subtract $60 - $40 = $20. Ben has $20 more than Joey.

27. **D** Mary has 3 pies. Each pie is cut into 6 pieces. To figure out the total number of pieces, you can multiply the 3 pies by the 6 pieces, (3×6). Mary eats 2 pieces. You have to subtract 2 pieces. The equation to represent the situation is $(3 \times 6) - 2$.

28. **A** To figure out the mass of the juice box, you have to add 24 plus 92 because the problem says that the juice box is 92 grams more than the brownie which is 24 grams. The answer is 116. $92 + 24 = 116$.

29.

	YES	NO
$3 \times \square = 6$		✔ $3 \times 4 \neq 6$
$6 \times \square = 24$	✔ $6 \times 4 = 24$	
$32 \div \square = 8$	✔ $32 \div 4 = 8$	
$42 \div \square = 7$		✔ $42 \div 4 \neq 7$

30. **B** The playground is in the shape of a rectangle. This means that opposite sides of the rectangle have the same length. You can add $35 + 35 + 60 + 60 = 190$.

31. **B and C** These shapes have four sides. Quadrilaterals are four-sided figures.

32. 4 more students chose dogs over cats. There were 3 students who chose cats, and 7 students who chose dogs. To figure out how many more students chose dogs than cats, subtract 3 from 7 to get 4.

33. **B** A square is also a rhombus.

34. **A and B** The x is located at $\frac{1}{4}$ on the number line. The whole unit is divided into 4 equal parts.

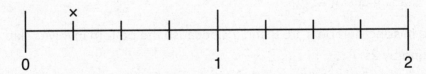

Choice A is divided into 4 equal parts. The mark indicates $\frac{1}{4}$. One out of the 4 segments is one fourth of the whole.

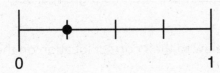

Choice B is divided into 8 equal parts. If you divide 8 into 4 equal parts it would be 2. The 2 represents $\frac{1}{4}$ of the whole divided into 8 equal segments.

35. **C** The total is $52. $31 and $9 are subtracted from $52. This can be written as $52 − $31 − $9 = $12.

36. **D** The associative property can be used to split the 6 × 4 into two groups.

$$(6 \times 2) + (6 \times 2)$$

$$12 \ + \ 12 = 24$$

37. **A** The figure below can be thought of as two rectangles made up of 4 × 5 = 20 and 3 × 2 = 6.

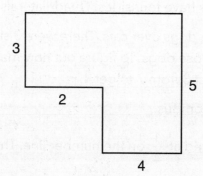

38. **B** 32 ÷ 4 = 8. 4 × 8 = 32.

39. **C** The missing numbers are 8 and 18 because the pattern involves skip counting by 2s.

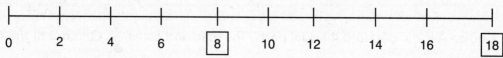

40. **D** The total of 36 is equally divided into 6 groups. 36 ÷ 6 = 6. Each child will get 6 gummy bears.

41. Write each fraction below to their correct location on the number line.

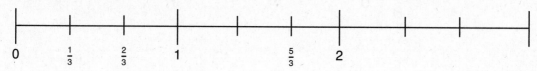

42. **True** When you compare two fractions with a numerator of 1, the fraction with the smaller denominator is larger.

43.

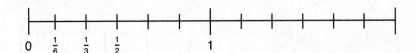

44. There are several ways to solve this problem. The shape can be thought of as a square. If one side is 4, then the other side has to equal 4. So an equation $n + 2 = 4$ can be used to find the value of n. $n = 4 - 2$. So $n = 2$.

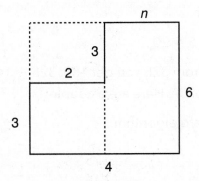

45. **B** The hour hand is at 6 and the minute hand is at 12. This makes it 6 o'clock.

46. **B** The eggs are arranged in an array of $2 \times 6 = 12$. This is the same as $6 + 6 = 12$.

47.

	TRUE	FALSE
$2 \times 8 = 16 + 2$		✔ $16 \neq 18$
$4 \times 5 = 2 \times 10$	✔ $20 = 20$	
$2 \times 4 = 16 \div 2$	✔ $8 = 8$	

48. Shade $\frac{1}{3}$ of the whole. The whole has been divided into 9 equal pieces.

3 of the 9 pieces make up $\frac{1}{3}$ of the whole.

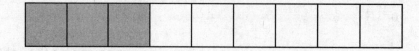

49. **B** One end is at $\frac{1}{2}$ inch and the other end is at 3. That is $2\frac{1}{2}$ inches long.

50. **B** Because $5 \times 5 = 25$.

51. **A** This is because $4 \times 5 = 20$.

52. **C** If you subtract 145 from 325 you get 180. $325 - 145 = 180$. There are many ways to solve this problem. Here are a couple:

You can use the standard algorithm.

$$\begin{array}{r} \overset{2}{\cancel{3}}\overset{12}{2}5 \\ -\ 145 \\ \hline 180 \end{array}$$

You could also break the problem into smaller chunks.

$$325 - 100 = 225$$

$$225 - 45 = 180$$

53. **C** Noelle has 5 stacks of quarters. This means she has $50 since each stack is worth $10 ($5 \times \$10 = \$50$). Angela has 8 stacks of quarters. This means he has $80 since $8 \times \$10 = \$80$. To figure out how much more money Angela has, you have to subtract $80 - \$50 = \$30$. Angela has $30 more than Noelle.

54. **A and C** You can think about the 4 pizzas as being made up of 4×8 slices. If Miguel ate 4 slices, you have to subtract 4 from the total number of slices. If you think about it this way, you can write it as $(4 \times 8) - 4$. However, if you thought about it as each pizza missing a slice because one was eaten, there are only 7 slices left in each pizza. Therefore, you can think about it as 4×7 slices.

Grade 3
Common Core Standards

APPENDIX
A

English Language Arts Standards

Reading: Literature (RL)
Key Ideas and Details
RL.3.1 Ask and answer questions to demonstrate understanding of a text, referring explicitly to the text as the basis for the answers.
RL.3.2 Recount stories, including fables, folktales, and myths from diverse cultures; determine the central message, lesson, or moral and explain how it is conveyed through key details in the text.
RL.3.3 Describe characters in a story (e.g., their traits, motivations, or feelings) and explain how their actions contribute to the sequence of events.
Craft and Structure
RL.3.4 Determine the meaning of words and phrases as they are used in a text, distinguishing literal from nonliteral language.
RL.3.5 Refer to parts of stories, dramas, and poems when writing or speaking about a text, using terms such as chapter, scene, and stanza; describe how each successive part builds on earlier sections.
RL.3.6 Distinguish their own point of view from that of the narrator or those of the characters.
Integration of Knowledge and Ideas
RL.3.7 Explain how specific aspects of a text's illustrations contribute to what is conveyed by the words in a story (e.g., create mood, emphasize aspects of a character or setting).
RL.3.8 (Not applicable to literature)

RL.3.9 Compare and contrast the themes, settings, and plots of stories written by the same author about the same or similar characters (e.g., in books from a series).

Range of Reading and Level of Text Complexity

RL.3.10 By the end of the year, read and comprehend literature, including stories, dramas, and poetry, at the high end of the grades 2–3 text complexity band independently and proficiently.

Reading: Informational Text (RI)

Key Ideas and Details

RI.3.1 Ask and answer questions to demonstrate understanding of a text, referring explicitly to the text as the basis for the answers.

RI.3.2 Determine the main idea of a text: recount the key details and explain how they support the main idea.

RI.3.3 Describe the relationship between a series of historical events, scientific ideas or concepts, or steps in technical procedures in a text, using language that pertains to time, sequence, and cause/effect.

Craft and Structure

RI.3.4 Determine the meaning of general academic and domain-specific words and phrases in a text relevant to a grade 3 topic or subject area.

RI.3.5 Use text features and search tools (e.g., key words, sidebars, hyperlinks) to locate information relevant to a given topic efficiently.

RI.3.6 Distinguish their own point of view from that of the author of a text.

Integration of Knowledge and Ideas

RI.3.7 Use information gained from illustrations (e.g., maps, photographs) and the words in a text to demonstrate understanding of the text (e.g., where, when, why, and how key events occur).

RI.3.8 Describe the logical connection between particular sentences and paragraphs in a text (e.g., comparison, cause/effect, first/second/third in a sequence).

RI.3.9 Compare and contrast the most important points and key details presented in two texts on the same topic.

Range of Reading and Level of Text Complexity

RI.3.10 By the end of the year, read and comprehend informational texts, including history/social studies, science, and technical texts, at the high end of the grades 2–3 text complexity band independently and proficiently.

Reading: Foundational Skills (RF)

Phonics and Word Recognition

RF.3.3 Know and apply grade-level phonics and word analysis skills in decoding words.

> **RF.3.3a** Identify and know the meaning of the most common prefixes and derivational suffixes.

> **RF.3.3b** Decode words with common Latin suffixes.

> **RF.3.3c** Decode multisyllable words.

> **RF.3.3d** Read grade-appropriate irregularly spelled words.

Fluency

RF.3.4 Read with sufficient accuracy and fluency to support comprehension.

> **RF.3.4a** Read on-level text with purpose and understanding.

> **RF.3.4b** Read on-level prose and poetry orally with accuracy, appropriate rate, and expression on successive readings.

> **RF.3.4c** Use context to confirm or self-correct word recognition and understanding, rereading as necessary.

Writing (W)
Text Types and Purposes
W.3.1 Write opinion pieces on topics or texts, supporting a point of view with reasons.   **W.3.1a** Introduce the topic or text they are writing about, state an opinion, and create an organizational structure that lists reasons.   **W.3.1b** Provide reasons that support the opinion.   **W.3.1c** Use linking words and phrases (e.g., because, therefore, since, for example) to connect opinion and reasons.   **W.3.1d** Provide a concluding statement or section.
W.3.2 Write informative/explanatory texts to examine a topic and convey ideas and information clearly.   **W.3.2a** Introduce a topic and group related information together; include illustrations when useful to aiding comprehension.   **W.3.2b** Develop the topic with facts, definitions, and details.   **W.3.2c** Use linking words and phrases (e.g., also, another, and, more, but) to connect ideas within categories of information.   **W.3.2d** Provide a concluding statement or section.
W.3.3 Write narratives to develop real or imagined experiences or events using effective technique, descriptive details, and clear event sequences.   **W.3.3a** Establish a situation and introduce a narrator and/or characters; organize an event sequence that unfolds naturally.   **W.3.3b** Use dialogue and descriptions of actions, thoughts, and feelings to develop experiences and events or show the response of characters to situations.   **W.3.3c** Use temporal words and phrases to signal event order.   **W.3.3d** Provide a sense of closure.
Production and Distribution of Writing
W.3.4 With guidance and support from adults, produce writing in which the development and organization are appropriate to task and purpose. (Grade-specific expectations for writing types are defined in standards 1–3 above.)

W.3.5 With guidance and support from peers and adults, develop and strengthen writing as needed by planning, revising, and editing. (Editing for conventions should demonstrate command of Language standards 1–3 up to and including grade 3.)

W.3.6 With guidance and support from adults, use technology to produce and publish writing (using keyboarding skills) as well as to interact and collaborate with others.

Research to Build and Present Knowledge

W.3.7 Conduct short research projects that build knowledge about a topic.

W.3.8 Recall information from experiences or gather information from print and digital sources; take brief notes on sources and sort evidence into provided categories.

W.3.9 (Begins in grade 4)

Range of Writing

W.3.10 Write routinely over extended time frames (time for research, reflection, and revision) and shorter time frames (a single sitting or a day or two) for a range of discipline-specific tasks, purposes, and audiences.

Speaking and Listening (SL)

Comprehension and Collaboration

SL.3.1 Engage effectively in a range of collaborative discussions (one-on-one, in groups, and teacher-led) with diverse partners on grade 3 topics and texts, building on others' ideas and expressing their own clearly.

    SL.3.1a Come to discussions prepared, having read or studied required material; explicitly draw on that preparation and other information known about the topic to explore ideas under discussion.

    SL.3.1b Follow agreed-upon rules for discussions (e.g., gaining the floor in respectful ways, listening to others with care, speaking one at a time about the topics and texts under discussion).

    SL.3.1c Ask questions to check understanding of information presented, stay on topic, and link their comments to the remarks of others.

    SL.3.1d Explain their own ideas and understanding in light of the discussion.

SL.3.2 Determine the main ideas and supporting details of a text read aloud or information presented in diverse media and formats, including visually, quantitatively, and orally.

SL.3.3 Ask and answer questions about information from a speaker, offering appropriate elaboration and detail.

Presentation of Knowledge and Ideas

SL.3.4 Report on a topic or text, tell a story, or recount an experience with appropriate facts and relevant, descriptive details, speaking clearly at an understandable pace.

SL.3.5 Create engaging audio recordings of stories or poems that demonstrate fluid reading at an understandable pace; add visual displays when appropriate to emphasize or enhance certain facts or details.

SL.3.6 Speak in complete sentences when appropriate to task and situation in order to provide requested detail or clarification. (See grade 3 Language standards 1 and 3 for specific expectations.)

Language (L)

Conventions of Standard English

L.3.1 Demonstrate command of the conventions of standard English grammar and usage when writing or speaking.

L.3.1a Explain the function of nouns, pronouns, verbs, adjectives, and adverbs in general and their functions in particular sentences.

L.3.1b Form and use regular and irregular plural nouns.

L.3.1c Use abstract nouns (e.g., childhood).

L.3.1d Form and use regular and irregular verbs.

L.3.1e Form and use the simple (e.g., I walked; I walk; I will walk) verb tenses.

L.3.1f Ensure subject-verb and pronoun-antecedent agreement.*

L.3.1g Form and use comparative and superlative adjectives and adverbs, and choose between them depending on what is to be modified.

L.3.1h Use coordinating and subordinating conjunctions.

L.3.1i Produce simple, compound, and complex sentences.

L.3.2 Demonstrate command of the conventions of standard English capitalization, punctuation, and spelling when writing.

L.3.2a Capitalize appropriate words in titles.

L.3.2b Use commas in addresses.

L.3.2c Use commas and quotation marks in dialogue.

L.3.2d Form and use possessives.

L.3.2e Use conventional spelling for high-frequency and other studied words and for adding suffixes to base words (e.g., sitting, smiled, cries, happiness).

L.3.2f Use spelling patterns and generalizations (e.g., word families, position-based spellings, syllable patterns, ending rules, meaningful word parts) in writing words.

L.3.2g Consult reference materials, including beginning dictionaries, as needed to check and correct spellings.

L.3.3 Use knowledge of language and its conventions when writing, speaking, reading, or listening.

L.3.3a Choose words and phrases for effect.*

L.3.3b Recognize and observe differences between the conventions of spoken and written standard English.

Vocabulary Acquisition and Use

L.3.4 Determine or clarify the meaning of unknown and multiple-meaning words and phrases based on grade 3 reading and content, choosing flexibly from a range of strategies.

L.3.4a Use sentence-level context as a clue to the meaning of a word or phrase.

L.3.4b Determine the meaning of the new word formed when a known affix is added to a known word (e.g., agreeable/disagreeable, comfortable/uncomfortable, care/careless, heat/preheat).

L.3.4c Use a known root word as a clue to the meaning of an unknown word with the same root (e.g., company, companion).

L.3.4d Use glossaries or beginning dictionaries, both print and digital, to determine or clarify the precise meaning of key words and phrases.

L.3.5 Demonstrate understanding of word relationships and nuances in word meanings.

> **L.3.5a** Distinguish the literal and nonliteral meanings of words and phrases in context (e.g., take steps).

> **L.3.5b** Identify real-life connections between words and their use (e.g., describe people who are friendly or helpful).

> **L.3.5c** Distinguish shades of meaning among related words that describe states of mind or degrees of certainty (e.g., knew, believed, suspected, heard, wondered).

L.3.6 Acquire and use accurately grade-appropriate conversational, general academic, and domain-specific words and phrases, including those that signal spatial and temporal relationships (e.g., After dinner that night we went looking for them).

Math Standards

Operations & Algebraic Thinking

Represent and Solve Problems Involving Multiplication and Division

3.OA.A.1 Interpret products of whole numbers, e.g., interpret 5×7 as the total number of objects in 5 groups of 7 objects each. For example, describe a context in which a total number of objects can be expressed as 5×7.

3.OA.A.2 Interpret whole-number quotients of whole numbers, e.g., interpret $56 \div 8$ as the number of objects in each share when 56 objects are partitioned equally into 8 shares, or as a number of shares when 56 objects are partitioned into equal shares of 8 objects each. For example, describe a context in which a number of shares or a number of groups can be expressed as $56 \div 8$.

3.OA.A.3 Use multiplication and division within 100 to solve word problems in situations involving equal groups, arrays, and measurement quantities, e.g., by using drawings and equations with a symbol for the unknown number to represent the problem.

3.OA.A.4 Determine the unknown whole number in a multiplication or division equation relating three whole numbers. For example, determine the unknown number that makes the equation true in each of the equations: $8 \times ? = 48$, $5 = ? \div 3$, $6 \times 6 = ?$

Understand Properties of Multiplication and the Relationship Between Multiplication and Division

3.OA.B.5 Apply properties of operations as strategies to multiply and divide. 2 Examples: If 6 × 4 = 24 is known, then 4 × 6 = 24 is also known. (Commutative property of multiplication.) 3 × 5 × 2 can be found by 3 × 5 = 15, then 15 × 2 = 30, or by 5 × 2 = 10, then 3 × 10 = 30. (Associative property of multiplication.) Knowing that 8 × 5 = 40 and 8 × 2 = 16, one can find 8 × 7 as 8 × (5 + 2) = (8 × 5) + (8 × 2) = 40 + 16 = 56. (Distributive property)

3.OA.B.6 Understand division as an unknown-factor problem. For example, find 32 ÷ 8 by finding the number that makes 32 when multiplied by 8.

Multiply and Divide within 100

3.OA.C.7 Fluently multiply and divide within 100, using strategies such as the relationship between multiplication and division (e.g., knowing that 8 × 5 = 40, one knows 40 ÷ 5 = 8) or properties of operations. By the end of Grade 3, know from memory all products of two one-digit numbers.

Solve Problems Involving the Four Operations, and Identify and Explain Patterns in Arithmetic

3.OA.D.8 Solve two-step word problems using the four operations. Represent these problems using equations with a letter standing for the unknown quantity. Assess the reasonableness of answers using mental computation and estimation strategies including rounding.

3.OA.D.9 Identify arithmetic patterns (including patterns in the addition table or multiplication table), and explain them using properties of operations. For example, observe that 4 times a number is always even, and explain why 4 times a number can be decomposed into two equal addends.

Number & Operations in Base Ten

Use Place Value Understanding and Properties of Operations to Perform Multi-Digit Arithmetic

3.NBT.A.1 Use place value understanding to round whole numbers to the nearest 10 or 100.

3.NBT.A.2 Fluently add and subtract within 1000 using strategies and algorithms based on place value, properties of operations, and/or the relationship between addition and subtraction.

3.NBT.A.3 Multiply one-digit whole numbers by multiples of 10 in the range 10–90 (e.g., 9 × 80, 5 × 60) using strategies based on place value and properties of operations.

Number & Operations—Fractions

Develop Understanding of Fractions as Numbers

3.NF.A.1 Understand a fraction $1/b$ as the quantity formed by 1 part when a whole is partitioned into b equal parts; understand a fraction a/b as the quantity formed by a parts of size $1/b$.

3.NF.A.2 Understand a fraction as a number on the number line; represent fractions on a number line diagram.

3.NF.A.2.A Represent a fraction $1/b$ on a number line diagram by defining the interval from 0 to 1 as the whole and partitioning it into b equal parts. Recognize that each part has size $1/b$ and that the endpoint of the part based at 0 locates the number $1/b$ on the number line.

3.NF.A.2.B Represent a fraction a/b on a number line diagram by marking off lengths $1/b$ from 0. Recognize that the resulting interval has size a/b and that its endpoint locates the number a/b on the number line.

3.NF.A.3 Explain equivalence of fractions in special cases, and compare fractions by reasoning about their size.

3.NF.A.3.A Understand two fractions as equivalent (equal) if they are the same size, or the same point on a number line.

3.NF.A.3.B Recognize and generate simple equivalent fractions, e.g., $1/2 = 2/4$, $4/6 = 2/3$. Explain why the fractions are equivalent, e.g., by using a visual fraction model.

3.NF.A.3.C Express whole numbers as fractions, and recognize fractions that are equivalent to whole numbers. Examples: Express 3 in the form $3 = 3/1$; recognize that $6/1 = 6$; locate $4/4$ and 1 at the same point of a number line diagram.

3.NF.A.3.D Compare two fractions with the same numerator or the same denominator by reasoning about their size. Recognize that comparisons are valid only when the two fractions refer to the same whole. Record the results of comparisons with the symbols >, =, or <, and justify the conclusions, e.g., by using a visual fraction model.

Measurement & Data

Solve Problems Involving Measurement and Estimation

3.MD.A.1 Tell and write time to the nearest minute and measure time intervals in minutes. Solve word problems involving addition and subtraction of time intervals in minutes, e.g., by representing the problem on a number line diagram.

3.MD.A.2 Measure and estimate liquid volumes and masses of objects using standard units of grams (g), kilograms (kg), and liters (l). Add, subtract, multiply, or divide to solve one-step word problems involving masses or volumes that are given in the same units, e.g., by using drawings (such as a beaker with a measurement scale) to represent the problem.

Represent and Interpret Data

3.MD.B.3 Draw a scaled picture graph and a scaled bar graph to represent a data set with several categories. Solve one- and two-step "how many more" and "how many less" problems using information presented in scaled bar graphs. For example, draw a bar graph in which each square in the bar graph might represent 5 pets.

3.MD.B.4 Generate measurement data by measuring lengths using rulers marked with halves and fourths of an inch. Show the data by making a line plot, where the horizontal scale is marked off in appropriate units—whole numbers, halves, or quarters.

Geometric Measurement: Understand Concepts of Area and Relate Area to Multiplication and to Addition

3.MD.C.5 Recognize area as an attribute of plane figures and understand concepts of area measurement.

3.MD.C.5.A A square with side length 1 unit, called "a unit square," is said to have "one square unit" of area, and can be used to measure area.

3.MD.C.5.B A plane figure which can be covered without gaps or overlaps by *n* unit squares is said to have an area of *n* square units.

3.MD.C.6 Measure areas by counting unit squares (square cm, square m, square in, square ft, and improvised units).

3.MD.C.7 Relate area to the operations of multiplication and addition.

3.MD.C.7.A Find the area of a rectangle with whole-number side lengths by tiling it, and show that the area is the same as would be found by multiplying the side lengths.

3.MD.C.7.B Multiply side lengths to find areas of rectangles with whole-number side lengths in the context of solving real world and mathematical problems, and represent whole-number products as rectangular areas in mathematical reasoning.

3.MD.C.7.C Use tiling to show in a concrete case that the area of a rectangle with whole-number side lengths a and $b + c$ is the sum of $a \times b$ and $a \times c$. Use area models to represent the distributive property in mathematical reasoning.

3.MD.C.7.D Recognize area as additive. Find areas of rectilinear figures by decomposing them into non-overlapping rectangles and adding the areas of the non-overlapping parts, applying this technique to solve real-world problems.

Geometric Measurement: Recognize Perimeter

3.MD.D.8 Solve real-world and mathematical problems involving perimeters of polygons, including finding the perimeter given the side lengths, finding an unknown side length, and exhibiting rectangles with the same perimeter and different areas or with the same area and different perimeters.

Measurement & Data

Reason with Shapes and Their Attributes

3.G.A.1 Understand that shapes in different categories (e.g., rhombuses, rectangles, and others) may share attributes (e.g., having four sides), and that the shared attributes can define a larger category (e.g., quadrilaterals). Recognize rhombuses, rectangles, and squares as examples of quadrilaterals, and draw examples of quadrilaterals that do not belong to any of these subcategories.

3.G.A.2 Partition shapes into parts with equal areas. Express the area of each part as a unit fraction of the whole. For example, partition a shape into 4 parts with equal area, and describe the area of each part as 1/4 of the area of the shape.

Standards for Mathematical Practice

The Standards for Mathematical Practice describe varieties of expertise that mathematics educators at all levels should seek to develop in their students. These practices rest on important "processes and proficiencies" with longstanding importance in mathematics education. The first of these are the NCTM process standards of problem solving, reasoning and proof, communication, representation, and connections. The second are the strands of mathematical proficiency specified in the National Research Council's report Adding It Up: adaptive reasoning, strategic competence, conceptual understanding (comprehension of mathematical concepts, operations and relations), procedural fluency (skill in carrying out procedures flexibly, accurately, efficiently and appropriately), and productive disposition (habitual inclination to see mathematics as sensible, useful, and worthwhile, coupled with a belief in diligence and one's own efficacy).

Standards in the Mathematical Practice Domains

1. CCSS.MATH.PRACTICE.MP1—Make sense of problems and persevere in solving them.

Mathematically proficient students start by explaining to themselves the meaning of a problem and looking for entry points to its solution. They analyze givens, constraints, relationships, and goals. They make conjectures about the form and meaning of the solution and plan a solution pathway rather than simply jumping into a solution attempt. They consider analogous problems, and try special cases and simpler forms of the original problem in order to gain insight into its solution. They monitor and evaluate their progress and change course if necessary. Older students might, depending on the context of the problem, transform algebraic expressions or change the viewing window on their graphing calculator to get the information they need. Mathematically proficient students can explain correspondences between equations, verbal descriptions, tables, and graphs or draw diagrams of important features and relationships, graph data, and search for regularity or trends. Younger students might rely on using concrete objects or pictures to help conceptualize and solve a problem. Mathematically proficient students check their answers to problems using a different method, and they continually ask themselves, "Does this make sense?" They can understand the approaches of others to solving complex problems and identify correspondences between different approaches.

2. CCSS.MATH.PRACTICE.MP2—Reason abstractly and quantitatively.

Mathematically proficient students make sense of quantities and their relationships in problem situations. They bring two complementary abilities to bear on problems involving quantitative relationships: the ability to decontextualize–to abstract a given situation and represent it symbolically and manipulate the representing symbols as if they have a life of their own, without necessarily attending to their referents–and the ability to contextualize, to pause as needed during the manipulation process in order to probe into the referents for the symbols involved. Quantitative reasoning entails habits of creating a coherent representation of the problem at hand; considering the units involved; attending to the meaning of quantities, not just how to compute them; and knowing and flexibly using different properties of operations and objects.

3. CCSS.MATH.PRACTICE.MP3—Construct viable arguments and critique the reasoning of others.

Mathematically proficient students understand and use stated assumptions, definitions, and previously established results in constructing arguments. They make conjectures and build a logical progression of statements to explore the truth of their conjectures. They are able to analyze situations by breaking them into cases, and can recognize and use counterexamples. They justify their conclusions, communicate them to others, and respond to the arguments of others. They reason inductively about data, making plausible arguments that take into account the context from which the data arose. Mathematically proficient students are also able to compare the effectiveness of two plausible arguments, distinguish correct logic or reasoning from that which is flawed, and–if there is a flaw in an argument–explain what it is. Elementary students can construct arguments using concrete referents such as objects, drawings, diagrams, and actions. Such arguments can make sense and be correct, even though they are not generalized or made formal until later grades. Later, students learn to determine domains to which an argument applies. Students at all grades can listen or read the arguments of others, decide whether they make sense, and ask useful questions to clarify or improve the arguments.

4. CCSS.MATH.PRACTICE.MP4—Model with mathematics.

Mathematically proficient students can apply the mathematics they know to solve problems arising in everyday life, society, and the workplace. In early grades, this might be as simple as writing an addition equation to describe a situation. In middle grades, a student might apply proportional reasoning to plan a school event or analyze a problem in the community. By high school, a student might use geometry to solve a design problem or use a function to describe how one quantity of interest depends on another. Mathematically proficient students who can apply what they know are comfortable making assumptions and approximations to simplify a complicated situation, realizing that these may need revision later. They are able to identify important quantities in a practical situation and map their relationships using such tools as diagrams, two-way tables, graphs, flowcharts, and formulas. They can analyze those relationships mathematically to draw conclusions. They routinely interpret their mathematical results in the context of the situation and reflect on whether the results make sense, possibly improving the model if it has not served its purpose.

5. CCSS.MATH.PRACTICE.MP5—Use appropriate tools strategically.

Mathematically proficient students consider the available tools when solving a mathematical problem. These tools might include pencil and paper, concrete models, a ruler, a protractor, a calculator, a spreadsheet, a computer algebra system, a statistical package, or dynamic geometry software. Proficient students are sufficiently familiar with tools appropriate for their grade or course to make sound decisions about when each of these tools might be helpful, recognizing both the insight to be gained and their limitations. For example, mathematically proficient high school students analyze graphs of functions and solutions generated using a graphing calculator. They detect possible errors by strategically using estimation and other mathematical knowledge. When making mathematical models, they know that technology can enable them to visualize the results of varying assumptions, explore consequences, and compare predictions with data. Mathematically proficient students at various grade levels are able to identify relevant external mathematical resources, such as digital content located on a website, and use them to pose or solve problems. They are able to use technological tools to explore and deepen their understanding of concepts.

6. CCSS.MATH.PRACTICE.MP6—Attend to precision.

Mathematically proficient students try to communicate precisely to others. They try to use clear definitions in discussion with others and in their own reasoning. They state the meaning of the symbols they choose, including using the equals sign consistently and appropriately. They are careful about specifying units of measure, and labeling axes to clarify the correspondence with quantities in a problem. They calculate accurately and efficiently, express numerical answers with a degree of precision appropriate for the problem context. In the elementary grades, students give carefully formulated explanations to each other. By the time they reach high school, they have learned to examine claims and make explicit use of definitions.

7. CCSS.MATH.PRACTICE.MP7—Look for and make use of structure.

Mathematically proficient students look closely to discern a pattern or structure. Young students, for example, might notice that three and seven more is the same amount as seven and three more, or they may sort a collection of shapes according to how many sides the shapes have. Later, students will see 7×8 equals the well-remembered $7 \times 5 + 7 \times 3$, in preparation for learning about the distributive property. In the expression $x^2 + 9x + 14$, older students can see the 14 as 2×7 and the 9 as $2 + 7$. They recognize the significance of an existing line in a geometric figure and can use the strategy of drawing an auxiliary line for solving problems. They also can step back for an overview and shift perspective. They can see complicated things, such as some algebraic expressions, as single objects or as being composed of several objects. For example, they can see $5 - 3(x - y)^2$ as 5 minus a positive number times a square and use that to realize that its value cannot be more than 5 for any real numbers x and y.

8. CCSS.MATH.PRACTICE.MP8—Look for and express regularity in repeated reasoning.

Mathematically proficient students notice if calculations are repeated, and look both for general methods and for shortcuts. Upper elementary students might notice when dividing 25 by 11 that they are repeating the same calculations over and over again, and conclude they have a repeating decimal. By paying attention to the calculation of slope as they repeatedly check whether points are on the line through (1, 2) with slope 3, middle school students might abstract the equation $(y - 2)/(x - 1) = 3$. Noticing the regularity in the way terms cancel when expanding $(x - 1)(x + 1)$, $(x - 1)(x^2 + x + 1)$, and $(x - 1)(x^3 + x^2 + x + 1)$ might lead them to the general formula for the sum of a geometric series. As they work to solve a problem, mathematically proficient students maintain oversight of the process, while attending to the details. They continually evaluate the reasonableness of their intermediate results.

Connecting the Standards for Mathematical Practice to the Standards for Mathematical Content

The Standards for Mathematical Practice describe ways in which developing student practitioners of the discipline of mathematics increasingly ought to engage with the subject matter as they grow in mathematical maturity and expertise throughout the elementary, middle, and high school years. Designers of curricula, assessments, and professional development should all attend to the need to connect the mathematical practices to mathematical content in mathematics instruction.

The Standards for Mathematical Content are a balanced combination of procedure and understanding. Expectations that begin with the word "understand" are often especially good opportunities to connect the practices to the content. Students who lack understanding of a topic may rely on procedures too heavily. Without a flexible base from which to work, they may be less likely to consider analogous problems, represent problems coherently, justify conclusions, apply the mathematics to practical situations, use technology mindfully to work with the mathematics, explain the mathematics accurately to other students, step back for an overview, or deviate from a known procedure to find a shortcut. In short, a lack of understanding effectively prevents a student from engaging in the mathematical practices.

In this respect, those content standards which set an expectation of understanding are potential "points of intersection" between the Standards for Mathematical Content and the Standards for Mathematical Practice. These points of intersection are intended to be weighted toward central and generative concepts in the school mathematics curriculum that most merit the time, resources, innovative energies, and focus necessary to qualitatively improve the curriculum, instruction, assessment, professional development, and student achievement in mathematics.

Index